ALONG MAIN LINES

THE "CORNISH RIVIERA"
G.W. Railway.

A DAVID & CHARLES BOOK
F&W Media International, Ltd 2011

David & Charles is an imprint
of F&W Media International, Ltd
Brunel House, Forde Close, Newton Abbot,
TQ12 4PU, UK

F&W Media International, Ltd is a subsidiary
of F+W Media, Inc.
4700 East Galbraith Road, Cincinnati,
OH 45236

First published in the UK in 2011
Copyright © Paul Atterbury 2011

Paul Atterbury has asserted his right to
be identified as author of this work in
accordance with the Copyright, Designs
and Patents Act, 1988.

A catalogue record for this book is available
from the British Library.

ISBN-13: 978-0-7153-3852-0
ISBN-10: 0-7153-3852-8

Printed in China by RR Donnelley
for F&W Media International, Ltd
Brunel House, Forde Close, Newton Abbot,
TQ12 4PU, UK

10 9 8 7 6 5 4 3 2 1

Produced for David & Charles by
OutHouse Publishing
Winchester, Hampshire SO22 5DS

For OutHouse Publishing
Project editor: Sue Gordon
Art editor: Dawn Terrey

For David & Charles
Acquisitions editor: Neil Baber
Editor: Verity Muir
Design manager: Sarah Clark
Production manager: Bev Richardson

F+W Media publishes high-quality books on
a wide range of subjects. For more great book
ideas visit: www.rubooks.co.uk

▶ Against a background of sidings filled with assorted goods traffic, including coal and military vehicles, the down South Wales Pullman passes slowly through Stoke Gifford in 1956. This scene, so expressive of the railways of that era, has all gone, and the site is now Bristol Parkway station.

ALONG MAIN LINES

PAUL ATTERBURY

David and Charles

CONTENTS

INTRODUCTION	6
MAINLINE MISCELLANY	8
Streamlining	10
Classic locos	12
Carriage interiors	16
Restaurant cars	24
Sleeper trains	32
Travel information	36
Timetables	38
Luggage & parcels	40
Lineside guides	42
Engineering	44
Container traffic	48
Air services	52
Motorail	54
Named trains	56
Railway hotels	62

SOUTHWEST ENGLAND	66
Train scenes	68
At the station	76
Famous places : Dawlish Warren	82
Tunnels, bridges & viaducts	84
Goods trains	86
Locomotive sheds	88
Railway works	90
SOUTHERN ENGLAND	92
Train scenes	94
London stations	100
Famous places : Clapham Junction	110
Tunnels, bridges & viaducts	112
Goods trains	114
Locomotive sheds	116
Railway works	118
WALES	120
Train scenes	122
At the station	126
Famous places : Barmouth Bridge	132
Tunnels, bridges & viaducts	134
Goods trains	136
Sheds & works	138

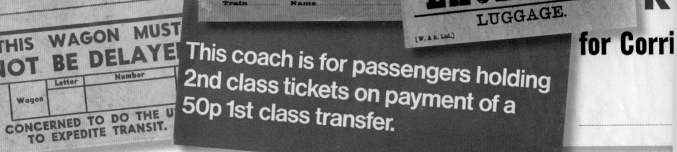

CENTRAL ENGLAND	140
Train scenes	142
At the station	148
Famous places : Monsal Dale	156
Tunnels, bridges & viaducts	158
Goods trains	160
Locomotive sheds	162
Railway works	164

EASTERN ENGLAND	166
Train scenes	168
At the station	172
Famous places : Harwich & Parkeston Quay	178
Tunnels, bridges & viaducts	180
Goods trains	182
Sheds & works	184

NORTHERN ENGLAND	186
Train scenes	188
At the station	194
Famous places : Shap Summit	200
Tunnels, bridges & viaducts	202

Goods trains	204
Locomotive sheds	206
Railway works	208

SCOTLAND	210
Train scenes	212
At the station	218
Famous places : The Forth Bridge	224
Tunnels, bridges & viaducts	226
Goods trains	228
Locomotive sheds	230
Railway works	232

LOST MAIN LINES	234
Across the network	236
The Great Central	242

INDEX	252
ACKNOWLEDGEMENTS	256

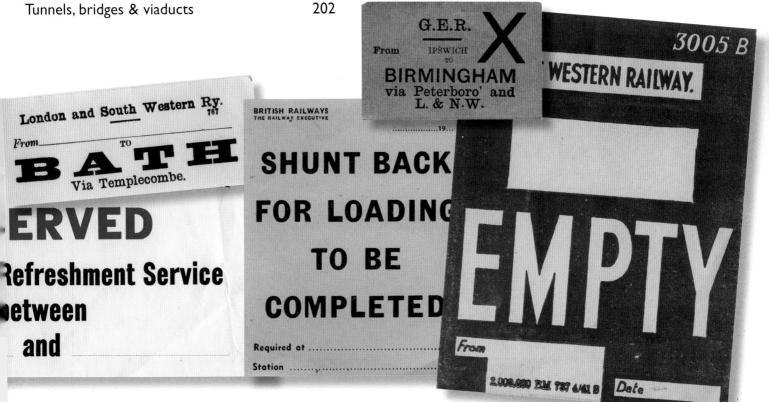

INTRODUCTION

Britain's railway network was built primarily to move goods and people quickly and efficiently over long distances, so the major trunk routes, and their important feeder lines, have always been the backbone of the system. The successful running of mainline railways has brought challenges for those operating them and thrills for those spectating – as generations of railway photographers, professional and amateur, have done their best to record. This book celebrates their achievement and, through photographs, postcards and ephemera, offers a rare insight into the mainline story.

▲ Somewhere in northern England, perhaps in the harsh winter of 1963, the railways are struggling to keep lines open and services running. It is a classic scene of the steam era.

▼ Placed at the very heart of the city, Edinburgh Waverley is an exciting station. Here, in this late 1960s view, a Deltic-hauled express is winding its way out of the platform.

WILLS'S CIGARETTES

HUMP YARDS AND RAILBRAKES, WHITEMOOR

▲ This 1930s cigarette card shows the LNER's massive goods yards at Whitemoor, near March in Cambridgeshire, one of England's biggest.

▼ Steam was still king when this old LMS Patriot Class locomotive No. 45519, 'Lady Godiva', headed a long train past Leeds City West signal box.

LEEDS CITY WEST

45519

In 1959 the locomotive shed at Aberbeeg, the Welsh Valleys, was largely equipped with heavy-duty tank locomotives built for the coal traffic that was then the core railway business.

▼ The London-bound Cambrian Coast Express pauses at Birmingham Snow Hill in 1957, giving a couple of trainspotters a fine view of Castle Class No. 5082, 'Swordfish'.

5 OCTOBER 1987 TO 13 MAY 1988

INTERCITY

▲ Eight Pullman services were still running in 1988, maintaining the traditions of speed, service and comfort that had been established a century before.

◀ In 1979, laden with new Ford Escorts and still open to the elements, a car transporter train enters Kilsby tunnel, Northamptonshire, hauled by a Class 87 electric locomotive.

▲ The restoration of St Pancras station and its development as an international terminus is proof that Britain's mainline railways have a future, as well as a past.

7

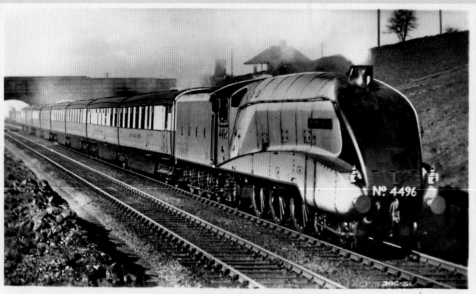

WEST RIDING LTD., POTTER BAR SOUTH.

ENTRANCE TO EUSTON STATION. 1904.

Express leaving Box Tunnel.

Largest Railwa

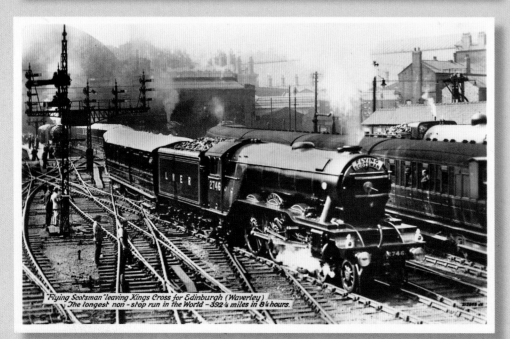

"Flying Scotsman" leaving Kings Cross for Edinburgh (Waverley)
The longest non-stop run in the World – 392¼ miles in 8¼ hours.

PENMAENMAWR VIADUCT

GANTRY SIGNALS, RUGBY.
L. & N.W. RAILWAY.

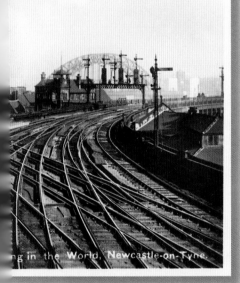

...g in the World, Newcastle-on-Tyne.

MAINLINE MISCELLANY

...OM THE SEA.

Midland Hotel
from Winter Gardens
Morecambe. 9507

STREAMLINING

During the 1930s, streamlining became a major concern of industrial designers, initially in the fields of aviation and motoring where, thanks in part to the use of wind tunnels, there was an increasing understanding of the relationship between speed and smooth, rounded forms. Soon railway companies all over mainland Europe and the USA, influenced by both practicality and fashion, were streamlining their locomotives. British companies were quick to follow, the LMS and the LNER taking the lead in the late 1930s.

▲ The streamlined Silver Jubilee service introduced by the LNER between London and Newcastle in 1935 was a great success, so two years later it was followed by the Coronation, linking London and Edinburgh.

▲ Competition between the East Coast and West Coast routes to the North went back to the Victorian era, and the battle was continued by the LMS and the LNER. In 1937 the LMS launched the famous Coronation Scot service, featuring a new class of streamlined locomotives designed by Stanier and finished in Caledonian blue with white lining to match the carriages.

▼ The LNER introduced its fleet of Gresley-designed A4 streamlined locomotives in 1935. In October 1938 'Mallard' became the most famous of the class by capturing the world speed record for a steam locomotive, 126mph. Unlike the LMS Coronations, the A4s retained their streamlining throughout their lives.

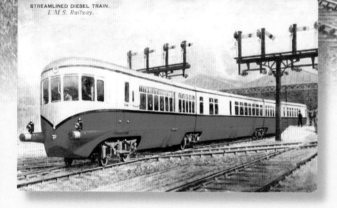
STREAMLINED DIESEL TRAIN.
L.M.S. Railway.

◄ Rounded forms influenced by German and French designs were exploited by a number of railway companies in the 1930s. Typical was this streamlined diesel set.

▲ Another, more revolutionary Gresley design, featuring a high-pressure water tube boiler, was the so-called Hush Hush locomotive, No. 10000. The unusual shape was determined partly by the nature of the boiler and partly by wind tunnel testing. Completed in 1929, the locomotive was tried out on a variety of services.

SOUTHERN
MIXED TRAFFIC LOCOMOTIVES
"Merchant Navy" Class

Naming Ceremony
OF
"P. & O."
AT
ASHFORD (Kent)
Thursday, 4th June, 1942
BY
Sir William Currie
Chairman
The Peninsular & Oriental Steam Navigation Company
accompanied by Southern Railway Chairman, Mr. R. Holland Martin, and
General Manager, Mr. E. J. Missenden

▲ Even the more traditional GWR flirted with a form of streamlining by adding rounded and flared details to conventional locomotives such as 'King Henry VII' and 'Manorbier Castle'. It looked clumsy and did not last long. This is 'King Henry VII' in 1936.

▶ Described as 'air-smoothed' rather than streamlined, the three classes of mixed-traffic Pacifics designed by Oliver Bulleid for the Southern Railway were the most numerous modern-look locomotives in Britain. First came the Merchant Navy class, from 1941 (right and above right), then the West Country and Battle of Britain classes. Unusual in both looks and mechanics, some worked until the end of steam.

CLASSIC LOCOS

▼ *From 1922, when the first went into service, Sir Nigel Gresley's A1 Pacific locomotives became the mainstay of the East Coast route to Scotland and other long-distance main lines. There were 79 in the class and all survived the LNER era into British Railways ownership, the last being withdrawn in 1966. From 1928 the class was rebuilt and renamed A3. The most famous, and only, survivor is 'Flying Scotsman'. Shown here is 'Royal Lancer'.*

Hundreds of locomotive types have contributed to the history of Britain's railways, and in each era some have been outstanding. Those included here, ranging in date from the 1920s to the 1980s, have made their mark for reasons of design, technical development, performance, reliability, longevity or simple popularity. Any such survey is bound to be subjective and incomplete, but all the locomotives illustrated here deserve their classic status.

▼ *This 1930s LNER photograph shows the meeting of two great locomotives – and two charismatic designs. On the left is the famous No. 1, the only survivor of Patrick Stirling's class of 53 express locomotives, built for the Great Northern Railway from 1870 and characterized by their 8ft 1in driving wheels. On the right is 'Sir Nigel Gresley', an equally famous locomotive bearing the name of the designer of the A4 Class of streamlined Pacifics, introduced on the LNER's express routes from 1935.*

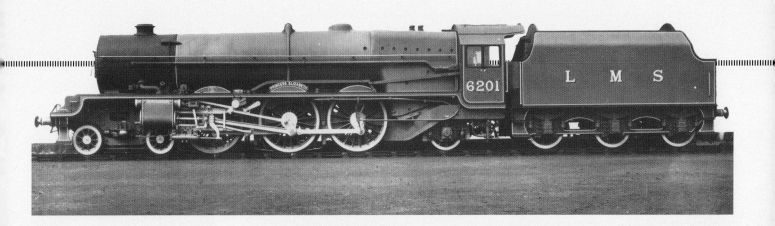

▲ The Princess Royal Class was the LMS's response to the LNER's Gresley Pacifics. Designed by Sir William Stanier for the West Coast route to Scotland, the first went into service in 1933. There were 13 in the class. This, the most famous is 'Princess Elizabeth', which gave the class its name.

▶ Also designed by Stanier, and famous as Britain's most powerful steam locomotive, the Princess Coronation Class was an enlarged and improved version of the Princess Royal Class. There were 38 in the class, built between 1937 and 1949. Early examples were streamlined, but by the British Railways era they all looked like this, No. 46244, 'King George VI'.

▼ Designed by CB Collett with the aim of bringing back to the GWR the title of 'Britain's most powerful locomotive', the King Class was introduced from 1927. There were 29 Kings, and all were withdrawn by 1962. The first, and most famous, was 'King George V', seen here leaving Paddington in 1960, still with the bell from its 1927 visit to the USA.

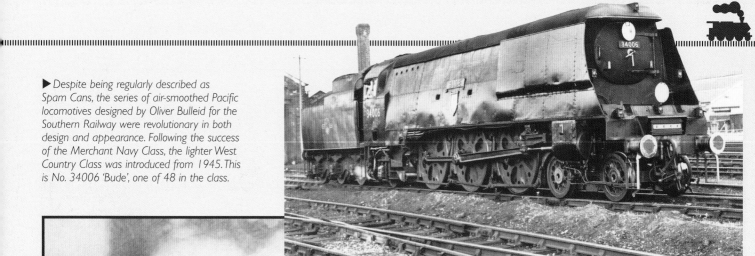

▶ Despite being regularly described as Spam Cans, the series of air-smoothed Pacific locomotives designed by Oliver Bulleid for the Southern Railway were revolutionary in both design and appearance. Following the success of the Merchant Navy Class, the lighter West Country Class was introduced from 1945. This is No. 34006 'Bude', one of 48 in the class.

◀ Designed by Richard Maunsell initially to haul the Southern Railway's heavy Continental boat trains, the Lord Nelson Class was introduced from 1926. The 16 members of the class, named after famous admirals, were destined for a long and influential life, with the last being withdrawn in 1962.

▼ In 1955 a prototype of what was to become the Class 55 diesel locomotive was developed by English Electric. Named 'Deltic' after its Napier engines and finished in a distinctive American-style livery, this operated on various British routes until 1961, by which time the 22 production Deltics were coming into service. Here it is at Doncaster in May 1960.

▼ In June 1977 a locomotive change from diesel to electric takes place at Crewe, as the Class 50 locomotive on a Glasgow-to-London train is replaced by Class 86, No. 86012. These two famous and long-lasting locomotive classes, both introduced in the 1960s, were important components in BR's modernization plans.

The shape of travel to come

InterCityAPT

Takes off between Glasgow, Preston and London Euston

InterCityAPT
The most Advanced Passenger Train

▲ One of the great might-have-beens of British Railways, the tilting Advanced Passenger Train was introduced on the West Coast main line in 1981. Technical problems caused a rapid withdrawal of the trains, and the project was abandoned.

▲ When introduced in 1976, the HST 125 train set, topped and tailed by a Class 43 diesel power car, was an immediate success and, over 30 years later, is still one of Britain's best and most popular high-speed trains. The 125s have worked in all parts of Britain. This one is en route from Penzance to Paddington in 1984.

▶ One of the most successful and long-lasting diesel locomotives on the British network, the Class 37 dates back to the late 1950s. Over 300 were built between then and the 1960s, and some are in service today. This classic maid-of-all-work has seen service all over Britain and many have been preserved. This 2001 photograph shows 37431 in BR Intercity livery.

CARRIAGE INTERIORS

From the 1890s, after a varied period of development, railway carriages became standardized as long, heavy vehicles with bogies, brakes, lighting, heating and lavatories. Compartments were open access or linked by a side corridor. There were infinite variations in design and decoration. Steel gradually replaced timber as the material used for the carriage body, but the body remained separate from the chassis until British Rail introduced integrally constructed carriages in the 1960s.

▶ *To anyone with a long memory, this classic view of a railway carriage compartment will be familiar. This is a promotional postcard issued by the LNWR showing a First Class compartment of the Edwardian era, but the details – the luggage rack, the pictures and mirrors, the curtains, the plush patterned upholstery, the antimacassars – did not change for decades.*

▼ *The first royal carriage was built in 1842 and was followed by many others, each more lavish in design and decoration than the last. This is Queen Alexandra's day saloon, in essence a mobile drawing room, in opulent Edwardian taste and complete with every comfort, including electric lighting and a fan.*

FIRST CLASS COMPARTMENT.
L. & N.W. SCOTCH EXPRESS.

▲ The most luxurious trains offered passengers various options. This is a First Class double compartment on the LNWR's American boat train in 1907, available to families or those requiring extra privacy on the journey between London and Liverpool.

▲ The open-plan carriage, with a central corridor, was an American idea imported into Britain during the 1870s. Unpopular at first, it soon became standard, particularly for Second and Third Class passengers and for suburban services. This is an LMS example from the 1920s, by which time the raised clerestory roof had virtually disappeared from use.

▲ There were lavatories on trains from the 1880s. Often ornamental in design, they had rather basic plumbing, namely a discharge directly onto the track. This is a Great Northern Railway example of the Edwardian era, fitted with a fold-down wash basin.

▶ Although lavishly appointed by modern standards, this is a Second Class compartment on the LNWR's American boat train. The carriage seen through the window, a kitchen car, shows the immaculate and complex external detailing typical of this era.

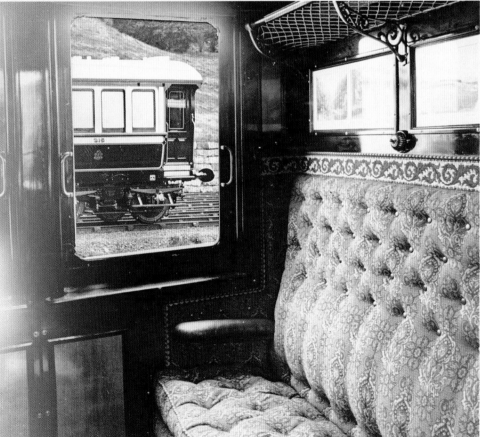

◀ *Another American idea was the club car, first used in Britain in 1895 and popular before World War I. The idea was that a group of season ticket holders or regular travellers should have exclusive use of carriages or compartments that were laid out in the style of a gentlemen's club. Later, the idea was used more generally, as in the lounge car seen here on the LMS's Royal Scot.*

▼ *Carriages were sometimes adapted for special purposes. As part of a move to improve passenger entertainment on long journeys, some were turned into cinemas, which became popular in the 1930s. This shows an LNER example, with blacked-out windows and raked seating. Later, they were more often used for staff training purposes.*

▶ *Following American practice, observation cars were first used in 1913. Regular use came later, on the LNER's Coronation express to Scotland in the late 1930s, on the Pullman Devon Belle between 1947 and 1954, and on routes in the Scottish Highlands during the 1960s.*

ALARM
PULL THE CHAIN
PENALTY FOR IMPROPER USE £25

▼ This is a First Class smoking compartment in a corridor carriage. Note the generously upholstered seats, cushions, curtains and foot rests, and the individual lighting and two-tier luggage racks.

▲ ▼ ▶ The four larger photographs on this page show different styles of LNER carriage interiors of the late 1930s. Above is a First Class smoking compartment in a non-corridor carriage, designed for shorter journeys but still boasting a carpet and antimacassars.

▼ This is the more basic version in the range, a Third Class smoking compartment in a non-corridor carriage. Although these are late 1930s designs, carriages similar to this remained in use well into the 1960s, particularly on suburban services, country routes and branch lines.

LADIES ONLY

WARNING
PLEASE MIND YOUR HEAD
WHEN LEAVING YOUR SEAT

THIS BLIND MUST NOT BE RAISED DURING BLACKOUT

◀ During World War II, trains, like buildings, had to be blacked out to protect them from enemy attack. Fitting Britain's carriage stock with blackout blinds was a huge undertaking.

▲ This is a Third Class compartment in a corridor carriage. Nevertheless, it is notable for the stylish Art Deco upholstery and the fold-down, padded arm rests.

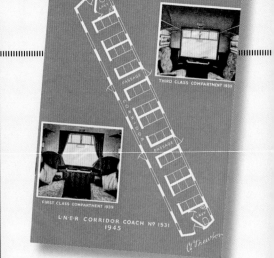

▲ This 1945 LNER brochure, asking passengers which designs they preferred, represented a simple kind of market research prior to creating a new range of standard carriages.

▲ Leather armchairs and an informal layout and atmosphere were the characteristics of club, or lounge, cars. This shows the Club Saloon on the LMS's Coronation Scot in the late 1930s.

▲ Pullmans – designed, built and operated by the Pullman Car Company – were always distinctive in appearance and fixtures. Notable were the light fittings, the marquetry panelling and the individual armchairs, which made the supplementary fare well worth paying.

◄ This delightfully posed GWR promotional photograph, showing very smartly dressed holidaymakers admiring the view of the river Tamar and the Royal Albert Bridge at Saltash on their way to Cornwall, is set in a typical Great Western corridor carriage of the 1930s.

FIRST

CAUTION
DO NOT LEAN OUT OF THE WINDOW

▲ By the 1950s, British Railways was producing simpler and more standardized carriages. This example of a compartment is basic, but has maps, information panels and pictures, mostly from the extensive range of topographical and architectural carriage prints made for BR.

▶ This Third Class open carriage with an offset corridor was built by British Railways for the suburban London-to-Southend service. The map and the flowery upholstery are the only decorative elements. Versions of the design were widely used in other regions.

▲ From 1951 British Railways introduced a new range of standard all-steel carriages, generally known as Mark 1s. This is a First Class compartment on composite-corridor stock, new in 1962. Wood veneer finishes, lighting, curtains and a mirror are echoes of pre-war elegance.

PLEASE CLOSE THE DOOR

▶ This 1958 photograph, issued by Cravens, the Sheffield-based carriage builder, shows a First Class open vehicle with offset corridor and reclining chairs. The mixed seating and table arrangement is now common throughout the modern network.

◄ The introduction of diesel multiple units on many routes from the 1950s also brought into being a new generation of simple, open-plan carriages with bus-type seating. These basic vehicles became universally familiar and offered passengers for the first time the chance to share the driver's view ahead.

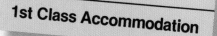

This accommodation may only be used by passengers holding 1st Class tickets.
Passengers holding 2nd Class Season tickets will be required to pay the **FULL** 1st class fare.

1st Class Accommodation

BR 29101/33

▼ This carefully posed 1958 publicity photograph shows passengers apparently enjoying the new open-style carriages on the Kent Coast line, in this case in Second Class. Carriages of this kind remained in service until the end of slam doors early in the 21st century.

▲ Another publicity photograph of the same era shows a lady demonstrating the reclining seat on an open First Class carriage in the new Mark 1 stock. Antimacassars and table lamps recall an earlier era.

Coach
P

▲ ▶ Since privatization, railway operating companies have leased their rolling stock from just a few suppliers, resulting in a general uniformity in carriage design. The styles and seating arrangements developed during the 1960s have been broadly maintained, though finish and detail vary from company to company. The photographs above, above right and below right show modern carriages in East Anglia, the West Country and Kent.

WELCOME ABOARD
AIR-CONDITIONED
INTER-CITY
The cool and quiet way to travel

▲ The Mark 2 carriage, with its fully integrated structure, came into service in the 1960s. The next decade saw the introduction of the Mark 2D, with full air conditioning. This 1971 folder promoted these carriages, which promised 'a new era in passenger comfort'.

RESTAURANT CARS

▼ *The Great Northern Railway pioneered the use of dining cars, and by the Edwardian era the dining car express was well established in the timetables of many companies. This card shows a famous example operated by the GNR.*

At first, station buffets were the main suppliers of food for passengers, and it was not until 1879 that the first dining car was introduced, by the Great Northern Railway. The development of trains with corridor connections was a significant advance, and restaurant and dining cars, with supporting kitchen and bar cars, were in common use by the end of the 1800s. Dining on trains became popular in the 20th century, and carriage interiors reflected fashionable styles. In later years, however, they saw a steady decline and eventually gave way to the now ubiquitous trolley.

THE LEEDS DINING CAR EXPRESS PASSING OVER WATERTROUGHS NEAR PETERBORO'

▼▶ *Passengers were used to bringing their own food, and some railway companies supplied picnic saloons. Below is an LNWR version. Picnic hampers could also be ordered in advance, as the GWR notice, above right, indicates.*

EXTERIOR THIRD CLASS PICNIC SALOON. L.&N.W. RAILWAY.

INTERIOR.

▲ *Full on-train dining facilities required additional heavy carriages and extra staff. This shows the staff for one LNWR restaurant car posing with the guard.*

ON CALEDONIAN RAILWAY. CORRIDOR COMPOSITE BRAKE CARRIAGE.

▶ *This promotional card issued by the Caledonian Railway in the early 1900s indicates the lavish interiors and table settings common in dining cars at the time.*

MIDLAND THIRD-CLASS DINING CAR.

THE BEST ROUTE FOR COMFORTABLE TRAVEL AND PICTURESQUE SCENERY.

◀ *Early dining cars were only for First Class passengers, but Second and Third Class versions soon appeared, as shown in this Midland Railway postcard of about 1910.*

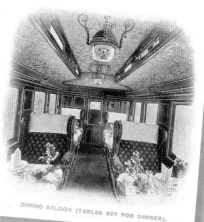

DINING SALOON (TABLES SET FOR DINNER).

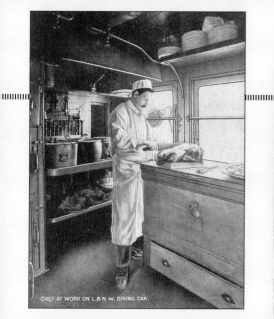

▲ Kitchen cars were a necessary adjunct to dining cars. These had to be fully equipped and well supplied with preparation and storage areas.

BUTLERS PANTRY.
L. & N.W. AMERICAN SPECIAL.

▲ The LNWR issued quantities of promotional Official Cards in the Edwardian era. Some of these offered 'behind the scenes' insights into the operation of dining cars, as well as advertising the de luxe American Special services that connected London with the trans-Atlantic liners sailing to and from Liverpool. This shows the butler's pantry. Note the knife sharpener in the bottom lefthand corner.

◄ The decoration of dining cars was generally reflective of current trends in interior design. This 1920s LNER example, broadly in the 18th-century French style that was popular at the time in hotels and ships, is carefully colour coordinated and features concealed lighting and salon-type chairs.

▼ Dining cars were often associated with fast, non-stop expresses and particularly with the boat trains serving the major international ports. This shows the dining saloon on the GWR's Ocean Express to Fishguard, notable for the decor of the carriage, the table settings and the flower arrangements.

THE DINING SALOON.
L. & N.W. AMERICAN SPECIAL.

▲ The kitchen and butler's pantry, shown at the top of this page, were the engine room for the elegantly decorated dining saloon on the LNWR's American Special services.

DINING SALOON,
"OCEAN EXPRESS."

▲ By the 1890s, dining cars were large and well appointed, often running on six-wheel bogies. This is a composite First and Third Class dining carriage built as Midland Scottish Joint Stock in 1893 to operate between London St Pancras and Glasgow.

▶ This unusually informal group is the dining car staff from a GWR Ocean Express, relaxing at Fishguard while they prepare for the return journey to Paddington.

▼ Early dining cars had kitchens with solid fuel cookers, which not only were difficult and demanding for the cooks but also posed a serious fire risk. Gas, often produced by the railways themselves and stored in tanks beneath the carriages, was used for lighting and gradually took over as the fuel for cooking. This is an LNER gas cooking range of about 1929.

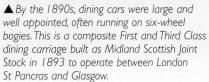

ALL-ELECTRIC KITCHEN CAR, "FLYING SCOTSMAN"

▲ All-electric kitchens first appeared in 1922, and from 1924 were used on the Flying Scotsman in the new all-steel vehicles. This cigarette card shows the electric kitchen designed by Gresley for the LNER. The carriages had generators and batteries. This kitchen could cater for 224 people at any one time. The card also reveals that a dining car carried 1,150 pieces of china and 350 tablecloths.

GREAT WESTERN RAILWAY.

DINING CAR.

(THIRD CLASS.)

First Meal.

FALMOUTH.

Menu
Fried Fillet of Whiting.
Roast Pork, Onions & Apple Sauce
"
Lamb Cutlets.
Potatoes.
Peas.

Sweets
Strawberry Sago Mould.
Baked Custard.
Apricot Cream.
Stewed Plums.
Cream.
Cheese & Biscuits.

See overleaf for particulars of Local G.W.R. Travel Facilities.

G.W.R.
Restaurant Car Routes

▲▶ The 1932 photograph above shows a typical GWR First Class dining saloon. The cutlery indicates that soup and three courses were served, plus dessert. Menus were decorative.

◀ This map, of a slightly earlier period, shows the routes on which the GWR operated dining cars. By then, most long-distance expresses, all over Britain, had dining cars.

▼ This LMS publicity photograph of about 1930 shows a standard Third Class dining car, apparently in a Highlands setting. Fixed seats were preferred both for safety reasons and to give diners some privacy.

▲ Dining cars were increasingly supported by lounge and bar cars, to encourage a feeling of ease and relaxation among passengers on long journeys. These were often decorated in a more contemporary style than the other carriages, and many echoed the design of ocean liners. This publicity photograph of the late 1930s shows the First Class lounge and cocktail bar on the LMS's Coronation Scot.

▼ This LNER bar car, which dates from the same era as the one shown above, is rather more basic, yet the overall look and the Bauhaus-inspired tubular steel furniture reveal a similar sense of stylish Art Deco modernism.

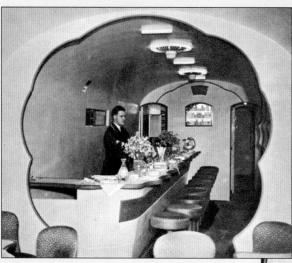

▲ The Southern Railway was influenced by 1930s modernism, particularly in its stations and railway buildings. This bar car was designed by Bulleid in a style influenced more by Hollywood than Germany. These images show that railway travel in the 1930s was perceived to be smart and modern, and it was marketed accordingly.

◀ Dining cars remained a regular feature of long-distance travel well into the 1980s. They then declined quite rapidly after privatization, becoming largely extinct by about 2005. This classic image from 1966 shows dinner being served on the Harwich Continental to Parkeston Quay.

▲ New Look meets Chanel in this British Railways publicity photograph showing a Pullman cocktail bar in about 1958.

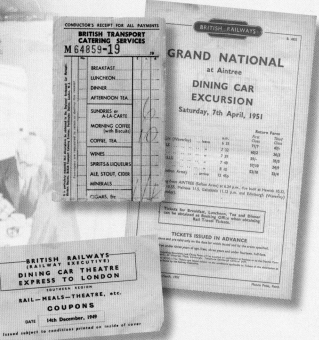

◀ The famous Blue Pullmans were introduced by BR's Western Region in 1960, serving Bristol and Wolverhampton. These all-Pullman diesel trains naturally included dining cars, shown here in the publicity brochure used to launch the service.

The Mid-Day Scot

Wine List

▲ Dining and bar car design generally echoed contemporary styles, but there were exceptions. In 1949 British Railways launched what they called Tavern Cars (top and above) on their Southern and Eastern regions. This attempt at bringing the pub onto the train reflected the increasing popularity of the informal buffet. The press release claimed the new Tavern Car 'combined the most modern features of restaurant and buffet cars with the traditional style of the Old English Tavern'.

▼ Another interpretation of 1960s modernism, with a slice of Scandinavia, inspired the design of the so-called Griddle Car for British Rail's all-electric Clacton-on-Sea service. By now, informality was the key word and the rise of the buffet car was inexorable, though dining cars were still popular, particularly for breakfast and tea. Eating habits were also changing, with people increasingly bringing their own food onto the train. Ironically, in a return to the early days of rail travel, this was often bought from the station buffet, which rose to the occasion by supplying packed meals.

BRITISH RAILWAYS   B.R. 21892

RESERVED
for Corridor Refreshment Service
between
and

For Parties and Excursions

From Railway Refreshment Rooms

packed meals

Afternoon Tea

38p

Assorted Sandwiches

Toasted Teacake

Fruit, Brown and White Bread and Butter

Fruit Cake or Swiss Roll

Biscuits

Preserves

Pot of Tea (*Indian*)

This Menu is Subject to Alteration without Notice.

Please ask for a bill and retain it

In case of difficulty please call for the Chief Steward. Comments will be welcomed by the Regional Train Catering Manager.

BUFFET CAR & SNACK BAR ON THIS EXCURSION

A NEW CONVENIENCE FOR YOUR COMFORT

A Buffet Car will run on this Excursion, so that whenever you feel like it, you can slip along the train and obtain a cold luncheon, tea, sandwiches, light refreshments, wines, spirits, beers, fruit or cigarettes. The list below gives an idea of what you can get

BUFFET CAR TARIFF ON EXCURSION TRAINS

Tea, Coffee or Cocoa	per cup	3d.
Pot of Tea or Coffee	per person	5d.
Tea and Bread and Butter (three pieces)		7d.
Bovril or Oxo (with Biscuits, 6d.)	per cup	4d.
Milk, Hot or Cold	per glass	4d.
Horlicks Malted Milk per glass 4d. (with added Milk)		
Ham	per portion	6d.
Meat Pies		1/-
Sausage Roll	each	3d.
Sandwiches		3d. & 4d.
Cheese, Biscuits and Butter	per portion	6d.
Roll and Butter		2d.
Pastries or Cake		3d.
Jam or Marmalade	per pot	3d.
Shortbread Biscuits	each	3d.
Biscuits	per packet	2d. & 3d.

WINES, SPIRITS, BEERS, ETC.

Sherry or Port	per glass	9d.
Vermouth, French or Italian		8d.
Brandy	per measure	10d.
Gin, London Dry		8d.
Whisky, Special		8d.
Gin and Vermouth	per glass	9d.
Bass, Worthington and Guinness	per bottle	7½d.
Dale's Cambridge Light Ale		5d.
Brown Ale		5d.
Double Stout		6½d.
Lager Beer		7½d.
Gaymer's Cydor (Large)		1/-
(Small)		7d.
Aerated Waters, Soda and Lemonade (Large)		6d.
(Small)		4d.
Ginger Beer		5d.
Dry Ginger Ale		6d.
Apollinaris Water	(Small)	6d.
(Baby)		4d.
"Presta" Grape Fruit		4d.
Lime Juice	per glass	3d.
Lemon Squash		4d.
Chocolates and Cigarettes		

London, April, 1934

L·N·E·R

Printed at the L·N·E·R Company's Printing Works, Stratford Market

SLEEPER TRAINS

In the early days, carriages were sometimes built with seats that could be altered for sleeping. It was not until the 1870s that dedicated sleeping cars, with proper berths, a lavatory and an attendant, were introduced. Pioneer users included the Great Northern Railway and the Great Western Railway, with the latter responsible for developing from the 1890s the type of sleeper still in use today, with shared or single compartments linked by a corridor. Routes expanded through the 20th century and well into the BR era, but today sleepers operate only from London to Scottish destinations and Cornwall.

▼ *By the Edwardian era, when this promotional postcard was produced, the sleeper was well established and First Class compartments, even those converted from day use, were lavishly decorated and equipped, with lighting, curtains, washing facilities and even pictures on the wall.*

SLEEPING BERTH. EAST COAST ROUTE.
The Shortest and Quickest between England and Scotland.

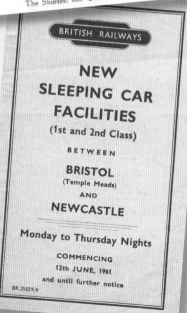

◄*In its heyday the British sleeper network criss-crossed the country to link many towns and cities. This 1961 leaflet promotes one such route. The 1976 BR national timetable lists over 130 destinations, many linked to motorail services, also at their peak then.*

▶ Once established, sleeper traffic became very competitive, particularly on routes between England and Scotland, and many railway companies designed and built fleets of sleeping cars, which they then promoted heavily. This Edwardian postcard shows vehicles built by the Caledonian Railway.

WEST COAST SLEEPING SALOON, CALEDONIAN (HIGHEST AWARD, ST. LOUIS EXHIBITION).

THIRD CLASS CORRIDOR CARRIAGE, CALEDONIAN.

◀▶ Sleeping car compartments varied from company to company. By the time the promotional photographs shown here and on the opposite page were taken for the LNER, First, Second and Third Class compartments were in use. Sharing was the norm in Second and Third, but the sexes were strictly segregated, unlike on the Continent. The 'models' in these delightful images were probably LNER staff. It is likely they are fully dressed beneath the blankets!

Please refrain from smoking in this sleeping compartment

▶ By the 1920s sleeping cars were becoming standardized, but there were many design and detail variations. This is an LMS example of that era, showing the by then familiar folding washing basin.

▲ Sleeping compartment design was greatly improved and simplified from the 1930s. This elegant LNER example reflects that and shows the influence of ocean liner styling. Today's sleeping compartments, though much more basic, echo similar design principles in their layout and equipment.

▶ Today only a few sleeper routes survive, mainly linking London and Scotland. However, the romance and the excitement live on, and there are many scheduled stops at remote stations. Here, on an early morning in 2010, Scotrail's Caledonian sleeper from London to Inverness pauses at Blair Atholl.

◄ This LNWR example, probably from the Edwardian era, shows a compartment in which the bed has been converted by the attendant from daytime seating – a style still in use on some overseas railways.

► From the 1970s sleeper routes were steadily reduced, but services continued to be stylishly promoted, as these 1977 and 1985 leaflets indicate. In 1985 there were still seven major routes, and not all were from London.

TRAVEL IN YOUR PYJAMAS

Until 1 May 1977

er-City Sleepers
make the going easy

INTERCITY SLEEPERS
NOW AVAILABLE WITH SAVER FARES
– EVEN CHEAPER WITH A RAILCARD

VALID FROM 30 SEPT 1985 UNTIL FURTHER NOTICE

We're getting there

TRAVEL INFORMATION

The rapid development of Britain's railways in the Victorian era made it possible for the first time for large numbers of people to travel for pleasure, and the railway companies were quick to exploit this aspect of their business. They were aware from the early days that, first, people needed to be encouraged to travel, and secondly, they would need help and guidance on the practical processes of train travel. The encouragement took the form of an ever-expanding mass of promotional literature. Guidance was offered through informative ticketing and clear identification of trains and carriages.

▲ The cost of travel was always a concern, prompting Government intervention during the 1840s to control ticket prices. Railway companies then began to offer all sorts of bargain and saver tickets. This 1930s independently produced leaflet offers a hire purchase scheme for season ticket buyers.

◀ Books and pamphlets describing railway journeys first appeared in the 1840s, and these set the scene for the great outpouring of promotional literature that has continued to the present day. British Railways was publicity conscious from the start, and particularly as competition from road traffic increased. This 1955 leaflet includes a network map and information aimed at all kinds of leisure travellers.

▼ The 'front line' for both passengers and railway companies was the ticket office, seen by both sides as the major source of travel information. This photograph shows a busy scene during the 1970s at the ticket office in a major station, with most people seeking information rather than buying tickets.

DEVON AND CORNISH DAYS
BY
E.P. LEIGH-BENNETT

Illustrated by
LEONARD RICHMOND, R.O.I., R.B.A.

◄ *Some railway companies became famous for their guide books, particularly in the 1920s and 1930s. This well-written and colourfully illustrated guide was published by the Southern Railway in the 1930s as a discreet promotion for their Atlantic Coast Express.*

E.R.O. 48841
O.P. 2

L M S
ALL SEATS RESERVED

British Railways

TRAVEL-BY-TRAIN
Passenger Facilities

SOUTHERN RAILWAY.

Train. | | Party. | | Class.

(a) M

ENGAGED

From | To
Date | Signature

PENALTY under Bye-Law 18 for UNAUTHORISED REMOVAL of this LABEL—£5

▼ *The departures and arrivals board was an important feature in every large station, often requiring good eyesight and careful interpretation. Until the 1970s these were usually mechanically operated, but since then electronics and digital displays have taken over. This shows the arrivals indicator board at Euston station in the early 1930s. It has echoes of a cricket score board, enlivened with enticing pictures of various popular destinations.*

London & North Eastern Railway (0.6127)

LIVERPOOL

Est. 1996 1M. 12/97

TRAIN ARRIVAL INDICATOR

TRAIN DUE	FROM			ARRIVES AT PLATFORM	MINUTES LATE
3-0	WOLVERHAMPTON	BIRMINGHAM	COVENTRY	2	0
3-5	TRING	WATFORD	AND INTERMEDIATE STATIONS	4	0
3-10	LIVERPOOL	BIRKENHEAD	CHESTER		0
	CENTRAL WALES	CREWE	STAFFORD		0
3-38	MORECAMBE	WHITEHAVEN	BLACKPOOL		0
	PRESTON	CREWE	RUGBY		0
3-45	THE LANCASTRIAN				0
	COLNE	MANCHESTER	STOCKPORT	STOKE	
4-5	CARLISLE	WINDERMERE	PRESTON	CHESTER	
	CREWE	RUGBY	NORTHAMPTON	BLETCHLEY	
4-21	BLETCHLEY	WATFORD			0
	INTERMEDIATE STATIONS				
2-36	NORTH WALES	CREWE	STAFFORD	1	0
	NUNEATON	RUGBY	NORTHAMPTON	BLETCHLEY	

TIMETABLES

Until the coming of the railways, time was a flexible concept, with variations all over the country. Railways had to establish standard time in order to operate timetabled services. Since then, timetables have been the backbone of railway life, enabling the planning of complex journeys and regularizing commerical and domestic life. Over the years these essentially functional documents have become quite decorative.

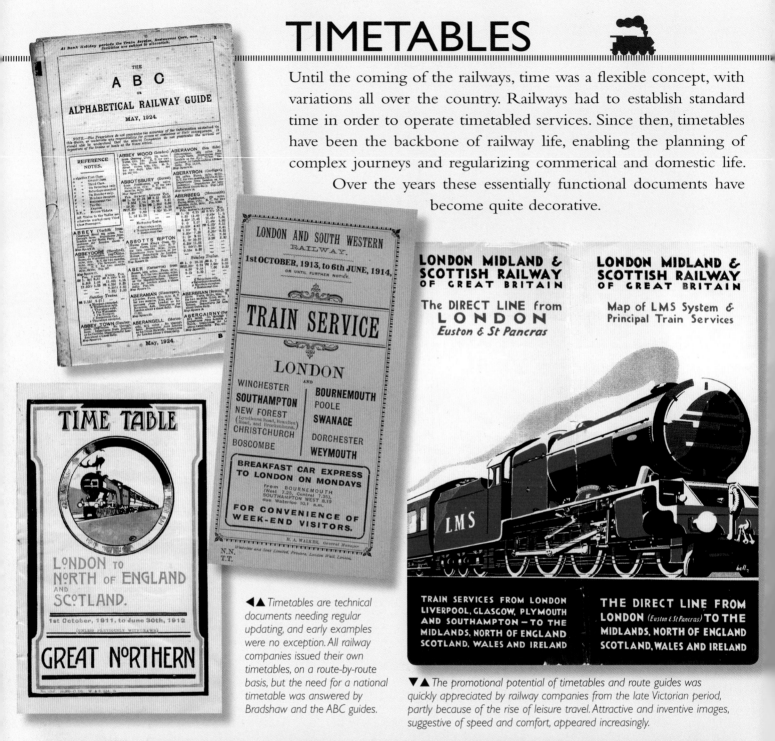

◀▲ Timetables are technical documents needing regular updating, and early examples were no exception. All railway companies issued their own timetables, on a route-by-route basis, but the need for a national timetable was answered by Bradshaw and the ABC guides.

▼▲ The promotional potential of timetables and route guides was quickly appreciated by railway companies from the late Victorian period, partly because of the rise of leisure travel. Attractive and inventive images, suggestive of speed and comfort, appeared increasingly.

WHITSUNTIDE

PRINCIPAL TRAINS
between
LONDON
and
YORKSHIRE
The NORTH of ENGLAND
and SCOTLAND

The Company reserves the right to cancel the train arrangements shown in this pamphlet, without notice, should it be necessary to do so

LNER

LNER

NIGHT TRAVEL
TICKETS
AT HALF FARES
To NORTH OF ENGLAND

3rd MAY 1937 until further notice

new and improved
diesel train services
in north east
scotland

**aberdeen
inverness**

12th JUNE TO 9th SEPTEMBER 1961

Passenger Timetable
5 May 1975 to 2 May 1976

Great Britain
Inter-City, local and suburban services
Irish, Channel Islands, Coastal services

▲ *In the 1930s the LNER was famous for its brand awareness and the use of contemporary design in its publicity material. Later, British Railways followed the same theme. These documents are all timetables, but are packaged so as to make them appealing to the customer, thus promoting particular routes.*

▼▶ *The transition from steam to diesel took a long time. Throughout the 1950s and 1960s British Railways used a range of timetable publications to promote the new diesel services as fast, clean, efficient and modern.*

TRAIN SERVICES

NE 16
BRITISH RAILWAYS

9th SEPTEMBER 1963 to 14th JUNE 1964

**HULL SHEFFIELD
DERBY BIRMINGHAM
BRISTOL**

At Bank and Public Holiday periods the train service is subject to alteration. For particulars, see other announcements
N.E. Region (9/63) BR 35032/11 Printed in Great Britain C & P

GNER

Guide to train services

London
Eastern Counties
Humberside
Yorkshire
North East
Scotland

NEW ...

EXPRESS DIESEL SERVICES
REFRESHMENT FACILITIES

between
BIRMINGHAM — CARDIFF — SWANSEA
(SNOW HILL)

commencing
MONDAY, 17TH JUNE, 1957

FREE ILLUSTRATED FOLDER FROM
ANY STATION, OFFICE OR AGENCY

BIRMINGHAM
(SNOW HILL)

STRATFORD-
UPON-AVON

GLOUCESTER
(CENTRAL)
CHELTENHAM SPA
(MALVERN ROAD)

LYDNEY

NEATH (GENERAL)   CHEPSTOW
NEWPORT   SEVERN TUNNEL
PORT TALBOT   JUNCTION
(GENERAL)
SWANSEA
(HIGH STREET)
BRIDGEND
CARDIFF
(GENERAL)

WESTERN REGION
BRITISH RAILWAYS

National Rail Timetable
28 September 2003 to Saturday 22 May 2004

Sunday 29 September 1996
to Saturday 31 May 1997

▶ *Privatization brought diversity back to timetables, with companies such as GNER taking great care of their corporate image. For a while the national network timetable, issued annually by BR, seemed under threat from the complexity of privatization and use of the internet. So far, however, it has survived, a tangible link with the railways' early days.*

National Rail
Britain's train companies working together

£10.00

39

LUGGAGE & PARCELS

The carriage of mail and parcels was until recently a core part of railway business, particularly in the days when the Post Office only handled letters. Mail travelled in dedicated carriages and trains, but parcels were often carried in the guard's vans of passenger trains. This continued until the Red Star service ended in the 1990s. Parcel traffic, including the sending of passengers' luggage in advance, required complex administration, generating copious paperwork.

SOUTHERN RAILWAY

These facilities apply ONLY to RAIL Passengers. Owners of luggage NOT travelling by MAIL will be required to pay the ordinary charges applicable.

PASSENGERS' LUGGAGE COLLECTED, CONVEYED and DELIVERED IN ADVANCE

IMPORTANT.

FILL IN THIS CONSIGNMENT NOTE and SEND IT TO THE STATION or HAND IT TO THE CARMAN.

RAILWAY TICKET(S) MUST BE PRODUCED BEFORE LUGGAGE CAN BE ACCEPTED.

G. W. R.
(1413 A)

LUGGAGE IN ADVANCE.

FROM

TO................................STATION

FOR STAMP

BR. 63/1

RLY. VIA

	No. of Passengers		Excess Charges to pay
	1st Class	3rd Class	

of these labels to be affixed to each package.

iva.—B.M. 60. 1947. (11) S.

TRAVEL CARE FREE
SEND YOUR LUGGAGE IN ADVANCE
ASK FOR DETAILS AT YOUR
LOCAL STATION

Manchester, South Junction, and Altrincham Railway.

110   Oxford Road Station, Manchester.

EXCESS LUGGAGE TICKET.

Received from _____ £ __ 8 for Excess Luggage to _____

per _____ Train _____

Gross Weight _____ lbs.

Allowance for _____ Passenger _____ lbs.

Weight Chargeable _____

Charged at _____ per lb.

Clerk's Signature _____

GREAT WESTERN RAILWAY. (5072)
2,500. W 122—Est. 315—9-26 S.

STATION FROM

STATION TO

TO BE DELIVERED BY SPECIAL MESSENGER.

		s.	d.
Special Delivery Charge	*PAID [debit sending Station]		
	*To be collected from Consignee		

* Erase line not applicable

BRITISH RAILWAYS
BR. 20910/2

COLLECTION OF "TO BE CALLED FOR" PACKAGES

"To be Called For" traffic, including passengers' luggage, will be released only upon proof of identity or authority to collect. These precautions are in the mutual interest of all concerned and your co-operation will be appreciated.

▲▶ *Still readily available to the collector is a wonderful variety of railway company paperwork relating to the carriage of parcels and passengers' luggage, and highlighting a now forgotten part of railway history. Colourful, and often obscurely worded, these documents indicate the complexity of the business in the pre-computer age.*

▶ *The regular carriage of the mail by train started in the 1830s, and the first travelling post office was in service by 1837. Mail trains then became an established part of the network. This photograph shows the interior of a sorting carriage in 1949, while the 1930s cigarette card gives such fascinating details as the average number of sacks sorted between London and Scotland – 1,040.*

PARCELS
MAILS

WILLS'S CIGARETTES

INTERIOR OF MAIL SORTING COACH

▲ Large stations had areas dedicated to the sorting, documenting and dispatching of parcels. This apparently unattended muddle is at Euston station in 1955. No doubt everything reached its destination eventually.

LONDON AND NORTH WESTERN RAILWAY.

POST CARD

THE L. & N.W.R. SERIES OF PICTORIAL POSTCARDS

(FOR ADDRESS ONLY.)

The Beach, Llandudno, from the Irish Sea and extends
BEST AND QUICKEST ROUTES TO
RHYL, LLANDUDNO, and the
Beauty Spots of NORTH WALES.
ABERYSTWYTH, BARMOUTH,
and the WELSH COAST.
CENTRAL WALES SPAS.
BLACKPOOL, MORECAMBE,
WINDERMERE, and the
LAKE DISTRICT.
The Highway to IRELAND via HOLYHEAD and
DUBLIN, and HOLYHEAD and GREENORE.
WEST COAST ROYAL MAIL ROUTE between
ENGLAND and SCOTLAND.

PARCELS
are received and forwarded
to all parts by
EXPRESS TRAINS
in Through Vans.

Prompt Collections and Deliveries.

Any information respecting Passengers
and Parcels Traffic may be obtained
from any L. & N. W. Office.

London and South Western Railway.

EASTLEIGH.
STATION.

PARCELS WITHOUT WAYBILLS.

DELIVERY NOT INCLUDED

LNER 2342/3/46—8,000   P. 3067
London & North Eastern Railway

PADDINGTON GOODS DEPOT

▲ In the 1950s the goods depot at Paddington station was heralded as one of the most up-to-date in the country, with modern handling facilities such as mobile cranes. Here, lines of parcels trains are being loaded with an astonishing variety of parcels and goods.

LONDON MIDLAND AND SCOTTISH RAILWAY COMPANY.

PARCELS FOR

MANCHESTER

(Via ANCOATS JUNCTION)   (VICTORIA)

From

FISH
by PASSENGER TRAIN
LONDON & NORTH EASTERN RAILWAY.

Date
From LOWESTOFT CENTRAL

TO LEEDS
G.N. Section   L.N.E. Coy.
VIA M. & G.N., SOUTH LYNN, WISBECH,
PETERBOROUGH & G.N.

Consignee
Owner and
No. of Wagon

Total
Sheets

SOUTHERN RAILWAY.

EGGS
WITH CARE.

◀ It is night-time in a large GWR station and trolleyloads of mailbags wait to be loaded. In the foreground, another trolley is piled with assorted packages for the scheduled parcels trains. Sometimes parcels and packages travelled by passenger train, greatly adding to the guard's workload and responsibilities.

LINESIDE GUIDES

As soon as railways appeared, books about them appeared too. Several date from the 1830s, generally describing the history and working details of the line as well as the route. The Railway Chronicle Travelling Charts, a series published in the 1840s, were probably the first lineside guides. They soon proliferated and, by the start of the 20th century, were being issued by the railway companies, with the GWR taking the lead. The Big Four – the SR, GWR, LMS and LNER – instigated ambitious publishing programmes. British Railways maintained the tradition, and the resulting flood of lineside guides was not to be stemmed, even by privatization.

◀▲▶ *Lineside guides, or route books, are colourful and decorative, with illustrations and some form of linear map. The 1930s examples often have the graphic qualities seen in railway posters of that era, while British Railways continued the tradition of adventurous design. Modern guides are more photographic but maintain the 'through the window' approach. Some feature walks, nearby pubs and places of interest.*

"WHO RUNS MAY READ"

LIVERPOOL
TO
LONDON (EUSTON)

Illustrated description
of the Journey

Along the Viking Border

LMS Route Book No. 2

PRICE ONE SHILLING

The RAIL TRAVELLERS' COMPANION

THE
**WEST
HIGHLAND
LINE**

SCOTRAIL

THROUGH 'WESTERN' WINDOWS

Features of interest
en route between

**PADDINGTON
& PENZANCE**

including the
TORBAY LINE

WESTERN REGION

"Through the Window"
PADDINGTON to PENZANCE
GREAT·WESTERN·RAILWAY
PRICE·ONE SHILLING

---

*Highlights
of your journey*

LONDON EUSTON   **MANCHESTER** PICCADILLY
BIRMINGHAM NEW STREET   **LIVERPOOL** LIME STREET

MANCHESTER
LIVERPOOL
WILMSLOW   STOCKPORT
RUNCORN   MACCLESFIELD
CREWE   STOKE-ON-TRENT
STAFFORD
WOLVERHAMPTON   LICHFIELD
    TAMWORTH
BIRMINGHAM   NUNEATON
COVENTRY
    RUGBY
    NORTHAMPTON
BLETCHLEY
WATFORD
LONDON

British Rail

DISCOVER
THE BEAUTY OF THE
North Wales Coast
on Britain's Scenic
Railway

UNTIL 2 OCTOBER 1988

Rheilffordd Gogledd Cymru

---

*Discover a World
of Difference*

THE BRISTOL TO WEYMOUTH LINE
REGIONAL RAILWAYS

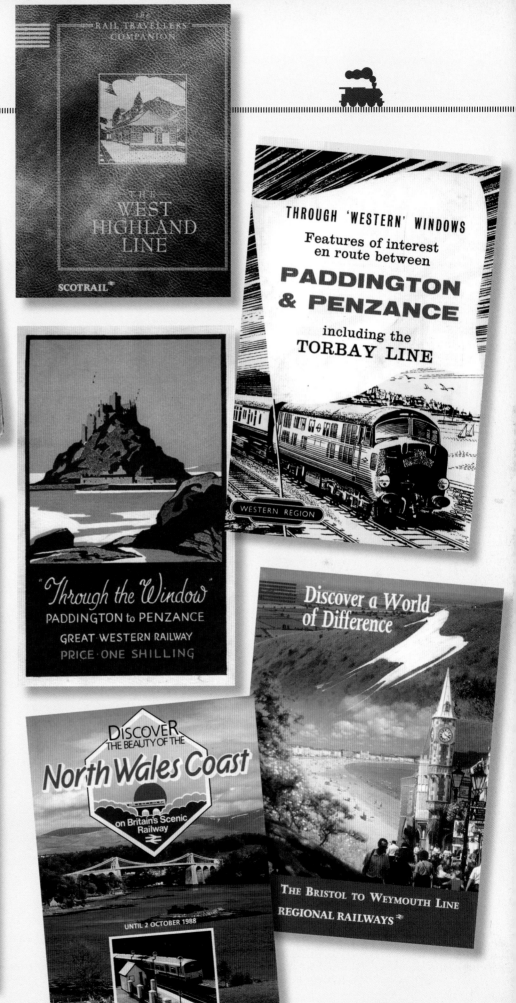

43

ENGINEERING

▼ *The railway network was still being developed in the 1950s, with track being doubled and larger bridges being built. Work was usually undertaken by the railways themselves. These pictures show 1930s bridge work: (below, top) a Southern Railway flyover to improve a junction; (bottom) an LNER replacement bridge over the river Aire.*

The building of the railway network in the 19th century was, above all, a triumph of engineering. All difficulties were seen as challenges to be overcome and, considering the nature of the workforce and the uncertainty of much of the technology of the time, the achievement was memorable. There is a great legacy of magnificent bridges, viaducts and tunnels, many of which are still in use. At the same time, there was a constant demand for maintenance, improvement and redevelopment.

▼ *Track requires constant maintenance and regular replacement. This 1930s cigarette card shows a mechanical track-laying machine in use on an LNER line. Such machines could re-lay 240 yards per hour.*

WILL'S CIGARETTES

MECHANICAL TRACK LAYER AT WORK

◀ The building of the Somerset & Dorset line south from Bath was famously difficult because of the terrain. The viaduct at Shepton Mallet, the highest of the seven that took the line through the Mendips, was completed in 1874 with a single track. This was soon found to be a bottleneck, so it was doubled in 1894.

▼ The painting of the Forth bridge is a well-known metaphor for work that can never be finished, and indeed this great steel structure did need regular repainting. This 1930s photograph shows a painting team working on a task that reputedly took seven years to complete.

▲ It was not uncommon for old tunnels to be opened out and replaced by deep cuttings. This shows the Hattersley tunnel on the Manchester-to-Glossop line being removed in the 1920s.

▶ One of the great engineering achievements of the 19th century was the building of the embankment along the South Devon coast near Dawlish. Before the century was out, heavy traffic had made it necessary to widen the track.

▶ In the early months of World War II the threat of bombing was taken very seriously, and most station train sheds had their glass removed – a wise precaution, as it turned out. This laborious process was carried out by hand, as seen in this photograph of London's Kings Cross station dated 10 July 1940.

▼ To minimize disruption, much maintenance and reconstruction work was carried out at night. In 1939 some platforms at Kings Cross were widened, and this photograph, taken in February of that year, shows the work under way. On the left, the Night Scotsman is ready to depart.

◄ *The breakdown train with its powerful steam crane was a vital part of the railway infrastructure, kept in readiness to deal with accidents and mishaps as well as engineering demands. This 1958 photograph shows the one at Corkerhill, Glasgow, with a Victorian Class 3F locomotive at its head.*

▶ *Electrification started before World War I and was considerably expanded in the 1930s. The long-distance routes came later, including Manchester to Sheffield in 1954 and London to Scotland in the 1970s.*

▼ *Though machinery was used whenever possible, the necessary basics of track maintenance were carried out by hand. Here, on a summer Sunday somewhere in the Midlands, a gang is distributing ballast, in a fairly leisurely manner.*

CONTAINER TRAFFIC

The idea of the container, as an independent box for the packing and transportation of freight, goes back at least to the 1850s, but its modern development starts in the 1920s with the door–to–door concept that linked rail and local road transport. British Railways took the idea further, and by 1957 over 35,000 containers of various types were in use. With the emphasis increasingly on speed, a number of dedicated services were introduced from 1959, including Condor and Speedfreight. These led to Freightliner, started in 1965, and the basis for the modern international container network.

▲ *The proliferation of container traffic in the 1930s is illustrated by this LMS correspondence card carrying a promotional image for their door-to-door service.*

▶ *The domestic market was very important from the 1920s. The major railway companies offered complete home removal services, using a combination of rail containers and local collection and delivery lorries. This shows a GWR example.*

THE RAILWAY CAN MOVE YOUR FURNITURE

Very low door-to-door rates
Expert Packers employed
Containers for safe and speedy transit

Please send details to your local Station Master, asking for a Representative to call

▲ *Home removal services were continued by British Railways through the 1950s and were widely advertised.*

▲◀ *The promotional card above was issued by the LMS in the 1930s to promote their door-to-door container services for both domestic and commercial markets. At its peak in that era, the door-to-door concept was in fact much older, as indicated by the steam lorry (left), built for container traffic.*

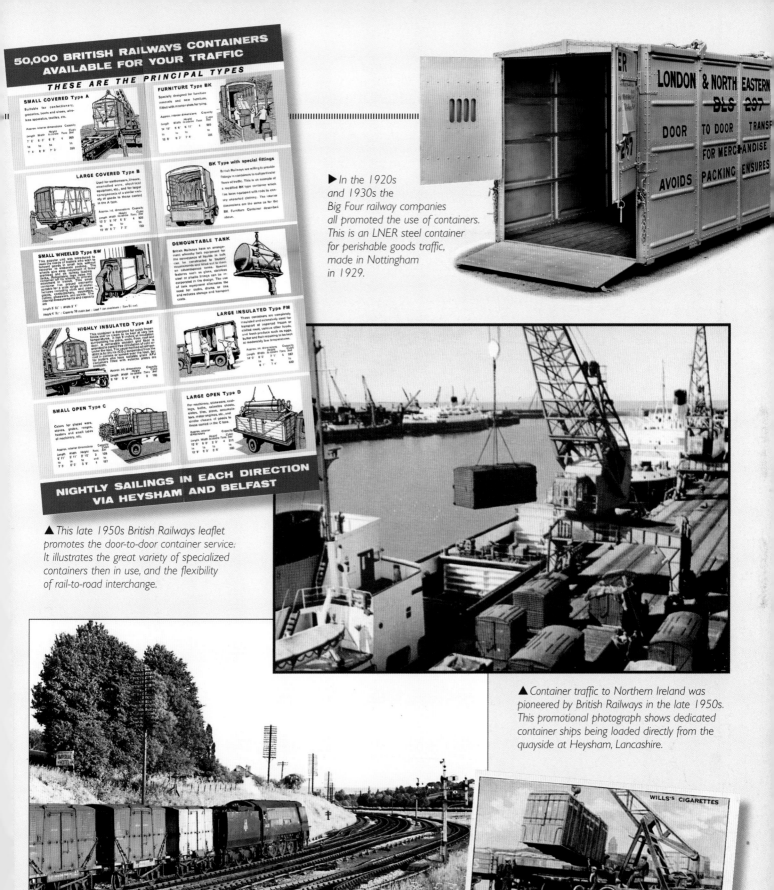

50,000 BRITISH RAILWAYS CONTAINERS AVAILABLE FOR YOUR TRAFFIC

THESE ARE THE PRINCIPAL TYPES

SMALL COVERED Type A

FURNITURE Type BK

LARGE COVERED Type B

BK Type with special fittings

SMALL WHEELED Type SW

DEMOUNTABLE TANK

HIGHLY INSULATED Type AF

LARGE INSULATED Type FM

SMALL OPEN Type C

LARGE OPEN Type D

NIGHTLY SAILINGS IN EACH DIRECTION VIA HEYSHAM AND BELFAST

▲ This late 1950s British Railways leaflet promotes the door-to-door container service. It illustrates the great variety of specialized containers then in use, and the flexibility of rail-to-road interchange.

▶ In the 1920s and 1930s the Big Four railway companies all promoted the use of containers. This is an LNER steel container for perishable goods traffic, made in Nottingham in 1929.

▲ Container traffic to Northern Ireland was pioneered by British Railways in the late 1950s. This promotional photograph shows dedicated container ships being loaded directly from the quayside at Heysham, Lancashire.

WILLS'S CIGARETTES

MOBILE CRANE HANDLING CONTAINER TRAFFIC

▲ The spread of container traffic required special handling facilities in goods yards. This 1930s cigarette card shows a mobile crane developed for this business.

▲ In 1959 a West Country Class locomotive hauls a fast freight of container wagons past Cowley Bridge, near Exeter – a familiar scene throughout the BR network at that time.

▼ In May 1965 a mixed freight, headed by an old LMS Patriot, No. 45531, 'Sir Frederick Harrison', drifts down from Shap Summit, in Cumbria. The first two flatbed wagons carry early Condor-type containers.

◄ In the 1960s great efforts were devoted to the development of container traffic. This shows the Dempster Sideloader, an experimental tank vehicle system made by the Powell Duffryn Group.

▶ The Roadrailer, developed in the early 1960s, was an attempt at making a container-style semi-trailer that could be adapted quickly from road to rail, and vice versa, without the usual interchange handling.

HOW THE ROADRAILER WORKS

1. Drives to factory as an articulated lorry.
2. Is loaded in usual way.
3. Drives by road to nearest railhead.
4. Road wheels retracted, rail wheels lowered.
5. Makes main journey as part of fast freight train.
6. Converted back to lorry completes delivery by road.

▼ The key to success was the efficient and quick interchange of containers between rail and road. The system shown here, with the containers supported on their own retractable rollers on raised rails, was briefly in use from the late 1950s.

From CARDIFF B.R. 21200/3
FREIGHTLINER TERMINAL
10-11-83
FREIGHTLINERS ...

To IPSWICH

Letter & Number	Load Cat.	Gross Weight of Contents
Wagon		
Container	H	Heaviest Single Lift

Contents
Consignee

◀▲ *Freightliner, introduced in 1965, was a dedicated container system built to international standards. Its network of scheduled high-speed routes and services linked a series of dedicated freight terminals, all fully equipped for mechanized container handling. The wagon label above came from the Cardiff terminal in 1983.*

▼ *Scheduled container services are the mainstay of freight traffic today, linking deep-sea ports such as Southampton, Felixstowe and Liverpool. Here, a Class 66 locomotive in EWS livery hauls a container train through the open landscape of northern England.*

Freightliner offers you ...

keenly competitive rates — fast, regular services
trouble-free transits — all-weather reliability
cheaper insurance coverage

Centres served by Freightliner in 1966, with fourteen new services in 1967 ▷

◀ *This Freightliner leaflet was issued in 1966 to promote a service that was still finding its feet. The map showed the way the network was being expanded, with new routes and terminals coming into operation in 1967.*

AIR SERVICES

In 1929, threatened with competition from the expanding domestic airlines, the railways obtained parliamentary powers to operate their own airlines. In 1934 the Big Four railway companies started Railway Air Services. The first route was Croydon to the Isle of Wight. Others soon followed, linking London and the West Country with cities such as Liverpool, Manchester, Glasgow and Belfast. The aim was control of the internal airline market. But World War II intervened.

▼ *Publicity material issued by Railway Air Services had a modern look, as befitted high-speed travel in the Art Deco era. The emphasis was on fast, reliable and comfortable travel, and on the inter-availability of tickets between air and rail.*

◀ *This 1935 promotional leaflet encouraged holidaymakers and others visiting the south coast of England to consider flying home. In some cases, rail tickets were valid for the flight.*

▼ *Railway Air Services was largely a feature of the 1930s, but was not forgotten in later decades. The 50th anniversary was celebrated in several ways, including this special First Day Cover issued by Benham's in 1984.*

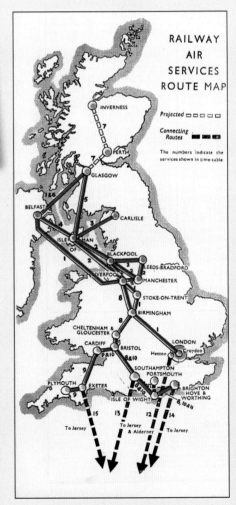

▲ *The network grew rapidly from 1934, as this map from a 1937 Railway Air Services timetable indicates. The main routes linked London with the Midlands and the North, but planned expansions to Southwest England and around Scotland, including the Highlands & Islands, were soon in place.*

◀ Railway Air Services quickly established itself as a mail carrier. In the early years some envelopes carried a stylish RAS symbol. This example was posted in August 1934.

▲ The mainstay of the RAS fleet was the twin-engined DH 84 Dragon, operated in conjunction with Imperial Airways. Some routes featured the larger, four-engined DH 86, shown here.

▲ During World War II most services ceased, but the railway companies retained their enthusiasm for running airlines. In 1944 there was a grand plan to develop air travel in postwar Europe, but with the formation of British Railways the desire to operate airlines disappeared. However, this 1948 brochure reflects some continuing interest, particularly in the area of joint ticketing.

◀ This summer 1939 timetable included details of 17 routes, along with the fares and freight rates. Children under three travelled free, adults were allowed 25lb of personal baggage, and livestock could be carried (suitably crated).

MOTORAIL

NEWS FOR MOTORISTS

•

"CAR AND DRIVER"
REDUCED RATES
BETWEEN SELECTED STATIONS
IN SCOTLAND
AND BETWEEN
SCOTLAND and ENGLAND

•

TAKE YOUR CAR BY TRAIN
AND AVOID
DRIVING STRAIN!

Early railways regularly transported private carriages on flat wagons, and when motor cars appeared the same system was used. Car transport by rail was formalized in the 1950s with scheduled services between London and Scotland, using trains comprising car carriers, either open or covered, and sleeping cars. In the 1960s the network was greatly expanded, with day and night services, and marketed as Motorail. By the early 1970s 100,000 cars were being carried each year, but traffic declined steadily and Motorail ended in the 1990s.

► For many decades vehicles were transported on flat wagons, but covered end-loading vans of the kind shown here were introduced in the 1950s. Double-deck transporter wagons were introduced from 1962, similar to those used for transporting new cars from the factories.

► A service between London and Fishguard, for the Rosslare ferry, was introduced in 1965. This British Rail publicity photograph of 1967 shows the Fishguard car carrier passing through Tilehurst on its way west.

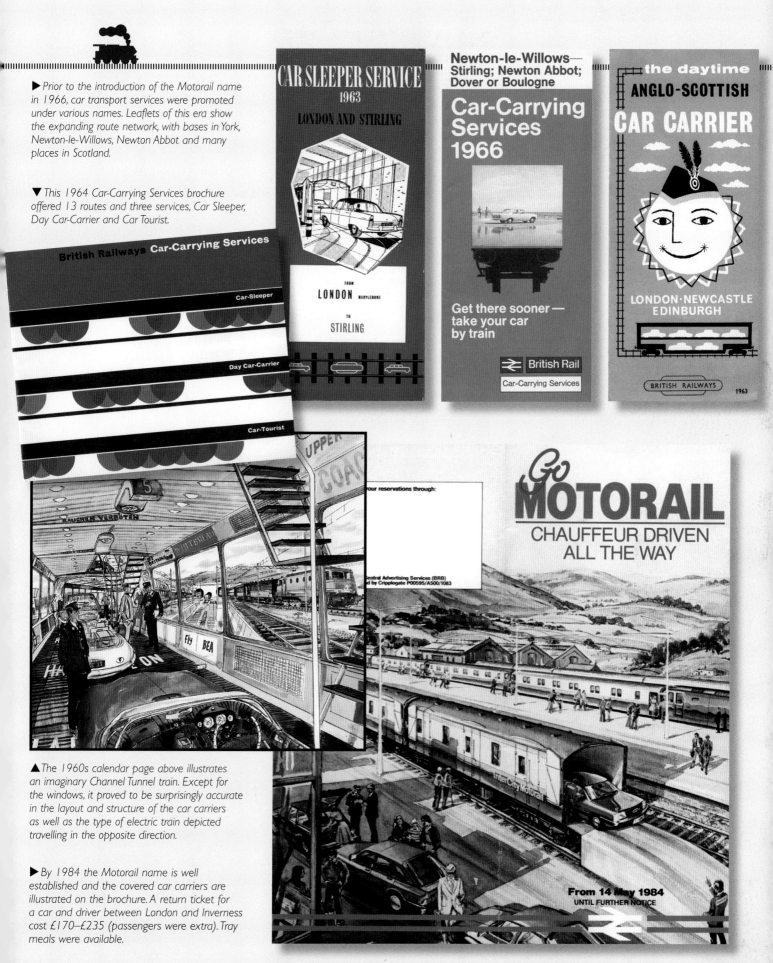

▶ Prior to the introduction of the Motorail name in 1966, car transport services were promoted under various names. Leaflets of this era show the expanding route network, with bases in York, Newton-le-Willows, Newton Abbot and many places in Scotland.

▼ This 1964 Car-Carrying Services brochure offered 13 routes and three services, Car Sleeper, Day Car-Carrier and Car Tourist.

British Railways **Car-Carrying Services**

Car-Sleeper

Day Car-Carrier

Car-Tourist

CAR SLEEPER SERVICE
1963
LONDON AND STIRLING

FROM
LONDON MARYLEBONE
TO
STIRLING

Newton-le-Willows—
Stirling; Newton Abbot;
Dover or Boulogne
Car-Carrying
Services
1966

Get there sooner —
take your car
by train

British Rail
Car-Carrying Services

the daytime
ANGLO-SCOTTISH
CAR CARRIER

LONDON·NEWCASTLE
EDINBURGH

BRITISH RAILWAYS   1963

your reservations through:

Central Advertising Services (BRB)
ed by Cripplegate P00595/A500/1083

Go
MOTORAIL
CHAUFFEUR DRIVEN
ALL THE WAY

InterCity Motorail

From 14 May 1984
UNTIL FURTHER NOTICE

▲ The 1960s calendar page above illustrates an imaginary Channel Tunnel train. Except for the windows, it proved to be surprisingly accurate in the layout and structure of the car carriers as well as the type of electric train depicted travelling in the opposite direction.

▶ By 1984 the Motorail name is well established and the covered car carriers are illustrated on the brochure. A return ticket for a car and driver between London and Inverness cost £170–£235 (passengers were extra). Tray meals were available.

NAMED TRAINS

The first named train was the Irish Mail, in 1848. After that, naming became an ad hoc process, with titles such as the Limited Express, the Club Train and the Sunny South Special being freely used. Naming became more meaningful in the 20th century, when titles like the Cornish Riviera Express, the Royal Scot and the Golden Arrow came into the timetables. The tradition continued into and beyond the BR era, with around 130 named trains recorded.

▲ The Cornish Riviera Express first ran to Penzance and Falmouth in 1904. It quickly became one of the GWR's most famous named trains, departing from Paddington at 10.30am daily. British Railways continued to run it into the diesel era.

▶ Although initially reluctant, British Railways soon introduced a new generation of named trains. This 1960 brochure described the 15 named trains then operated by BR's Western Region, who promoted them with their 'romantic titles and distinctive livery'.

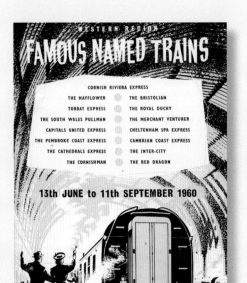

WESTERN REGION
FAMOUS NAMED TRAINS

CORNISH RIVIERA EXPRESS

THE MAYFLOWER	THE BRISTOLIAN
THE TORBAY EXPRESS	THE ROYAL DUCHY
THE SOUTH WALES PULLMAN	THE MERCHANT VENTURER
CAPITALS UNITED EXPRESS	CHELTENHAM SPA EXPRESS
THE PEMBROKE COAST EXPRESS	CAMBRIAN COAST EXPRESS
THE CATHEDRALS EXPRESS	THE INTER-CITY
THE CORNISHMAN	THE RED DRAGON

13th JUNE to 11th SEPTEMBER 1960

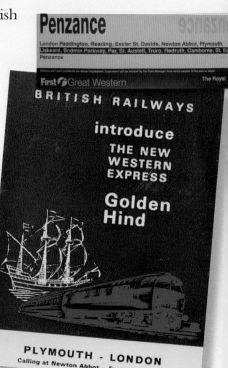

Penzance
London Paddington, Reading, Exeter St. Davids, Newton Abbot, Plymouth, Liskeard, Bodmin Parkway, Par, St. Austell, Truro, Redruth, Camborne, St. Er, Penzance

First Great Western   The Royal

BRITISH RAILWAYS

introduce
THE NEW
WESTERN
EXPRESS

Golden Hind

PLYMOUTH - LONDON
Calling at Newton Abbot · Exeter · Taunton

▲ British Railways liked names with historical or regional associations. Typical was the Golden Hind, between London and Plymouth, described in this promotional brochure as 'an elite train'. The name Golden Hind has recently been used by First Great Western, as has The Royal Duchy.

Famous Train Journeys No. 2
DEVON BELLE
ALAN ANDERSON

▲▶ Introduced in 1947, the Devon Belle was an all-Pullman service linking London with Plymouth and Ilfracombe. Its popularity was celebrated in books, and it was regularly hauled by Merchant Navy Class locomotives such as No. 35008, 'Orient Line'.

▲ The Ocean Liner Express was a boat train service linking London and Southampton docks. Here, in the 1960s, West Country Class locomotive No. 34098, 'Templecombe', makes a very smoky departure.

▶ Introduced as the Southern Belle in 1908, the Brighton Belle became, uniquely, an all-electric Pullman train from 1933. The final day of this much-loved train, Sunday 30 April 1972, was widely commemorated.

Farewell to the
BRIGHTON BELLE
Sunday 30 April 1972

A free black and white print of this picture can be obtained by sending 3p stamp to the Public Relations & Publicity Officer (Dept RWR), British Rail, Southern Region, Waterloo Station, London, SE1.

≷ Southern

▲ 1972 also saw the last run of the Golden Arrow. The most famous of all intercontinental expresses, it had been in the timetable since 1929. This 1963 publicity photograph shows passengers bound for Paris boarding the Pullman cars at London Victoria.

▲ The last dedicated mainline Pullman trains, the diesel-electric powered Blue Pullman train sets, were introduced by British Railways in 1960. There were several routes, operated by the Western and Midland regions. This shows the Midland Pullman, which linked Manchester, Leicester and London between 1960 and 1966.

▼ In 1921 the GWR introduced an express service from London to Aberystwyth via Shrewsbury. In 1927 this was named the Cambrian Coast Express, and it continued to run in one form or another until 1991. This shows the train in the 1950s, in the care of a well-turned out GWR Manor Class locomotive, No. 7818, 'Granville Manor'.

The IRISH MAIL
LONDON — HOLYHEAD — DUBLIN

▲ The first named train, dating from 1848, the Irish Mail was still running between London and Holyhead over a century later. It was celebrated in this 1960s book, in a series entitled 'Famous Trains and Their Routes'.

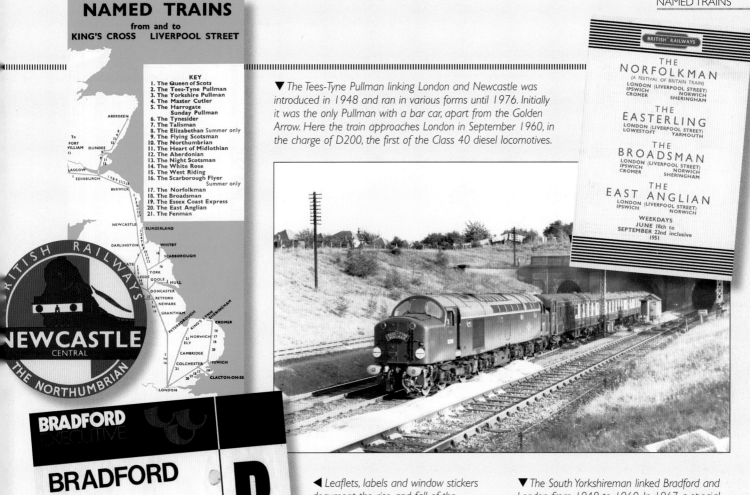

NAMED TRAINS
from and to
KING'S CROSS   LIVERPOOL STREET

KEY
1. The Queen of Scots
2. The Tees-Tyne Pullman
3. The Yorkshire Pullman
4. The Master Cutler
5. The Harrogate
    Sunday Pullman
6. The Tynesider
7. The Talisman
8. The Elizabethan Summer only
9. The Flying Scotsman
10. The Northumbrian
11. The Heart of Midlothian
12. The Aberdonian
13. The Night Scotsman
14. The White Rose
15. The West Riding
16. The Scarborough Flyer
    Summer only
17. The Norfolkman
18. The Broadsman
19. The Essex Coast Express
20. The East Anglian
21. The Fenman

BRITISH RAILWAYS

THE NORFOLKMAN
(A FESTIVAL OF BRITAIN TRAIN)
LONDON (LIVERPOOL STREET)
IPSWICH   NORWICH
CROMER   SHERINGHAM

THE EASTERLING
LONDON (LIVERPOOL STREET)
LOWESTOFT   YARMOUTH

THE BROADSMAN
LONDON (LIVERPOOL STREET)
IPSWICH   NORWICH
CROMER   SHERINGHAM

THE EAST ANGLIAN
LONDON (LIVERPOOL STREET)
IPSWICH   NORWICH

WEEKDAYS
JUNE 18th to
SEPTEMBER 22nd inclusive
1951

▼ *The Tees-Tyne Pullman linking London and Newcastle was introduced in 1948 and ran in various forms until 1976. Initially it was the only Pullman with a bar car, apart from the Golden Arrow. Here the train approaches London in September 1960, in the charge of D200, the first of the Class 40 diesel locomotives.*

BRADFORD EXECUTIVE

BRADFORD
via
Doncaster
Wakefield Westgate
New Pudsey

B

◄ *Leaflets, labels and window stickers document the rise and fall of the named train in the East and North of England during the BR years.*

▼ *The South Yorkshireman linked Bradford and London from 1948 to 1960. In 1967 a special, bearing the South Yorkshireman headboard and hauled by Jubilee No. 45562, 'Alberta', paused for a photograph at Carnforth, while the bowler-hatted stationmaster looked on.*

▲ In 1959 steam was still dominant, and the famous A4s were often to be seen heading the Scarborough Flyer, photographed here passing Hadley Wood on the way into London, headed by No. 60033, 'Seagull'. The Scarborough Flyer name has recently been applied to special trains on the route hauled by preserved steam locomotives.

NAMED TRAINS ON THE EAST COAST MAIN LINE

The Tynesider
The Talisman
The Flying Scotsman
The Queen of Scots
The Northumbrian
The Heart of Midlothian
The Tees-Tyne Pullman
The Aberdonian
The Night Scotsman

Weekdays
17th June to
7th September, 1963

BRITISH RAILWAYS

Famous trains N°1
THE ELIZABETHAN

9ᴅ AN Ian Allan PUBLICATION

the **RED ROSE**
BRITISH RAILWAYS

EACH WEEKDAY BETWEEN
EUSTON and **LIVERPOOL**

◀▲ In the 1950s and 1960s British Railways operated a large number of named trains throughout the regions. Numerous brochures and booklets were produced by BR to promote these services. Others were published independently, for the enthusiast, including the Ian Allan 'Famous Trains' series, dating from the late 1950s.

THE ABERDONIAN

ABERDEEN

via
Darlington
Newcastle
Kirkcaldy
Arbroath

Stonehaven
Edinburgh
Dundee
Montrose

E

▲ There were many named trains on London-to-Scotland East Coast and West Coast services, some of which, including the Flying Scotsman or the Coronation Scot, are part of railway history. There were others less well known, including the Elizabethan and the Caledonian, a service linking London and Glasgow. The locomotive heading the train here is Princess Coronation Class No. 46244, 'King George VI'.

BRITISH RAILWAYS

GLASGOW
QUEEN STREET

THE NORTH BRITON

▶ In September 1961 a Class 40 diesel hauls the Royal Scot past Quintinshill signal box, near Gretna Green, on its way north. It was here, on 22 May 1915, that the worst train disaster in British railway history took place. There were 227 fatalities and 246 injured, mostly soldiers on their way to join the fighting in Gallipoli.

RAILWAY HOTELS

Railway companies, quick to appreciate the needs of travellers, began to build hotels in the late 1830s, and by the 1850s the pattern of having a large hotel adjacent to, or as part of, a major station was established. Railway hotels were built all over Britain, in cities, towns, ports and resorts, often in adventurous or extravagant architectural styles, from the Victorian period to the 1930s. In 1901 there were 61 railway-owned hotels in Britain. Now there are none.

▼ *There are railway hotels all over Britain that are nothing to do with railway companies. This one, in Dorset, features a splendid ceramic tile panel of a Southern Railway locomotive.*

Tregenna Castle Hotel, St Ives, Cornwall

▲ *The GWR bought Tregenna Castle, near St Ives in Cornwall, in 1878 and turned it into a lavish hotel with its own golf course. This aerial view shows the hotel in the early 1960s, when it was one of 37 in the care of British Transport Hotels, a division of British Railways.*

▲ *Another GWR purchase was the Manor House Hotel, near Moretonhampstead in Devon, in 1929, seen as a country house hotel with great potential, despite being at the end of a branch line.*

GOLF (EIGHTEEN HOLES)

TENNIS · BADMINTON · SQUASH · RIVER FISHING · RIDING

Manor House Hotel
MORETONHAMPSTEAD. DEVON

CANNON STREET STATION & HOTEL
SOUTH EASTERN & CHATHAM RY.

◄ *In the early 1960s British Transport Hotels produced a promotional calendar, illustrated with contemporary drawings highlighting selected hotels.*

▲ *Most London termini had their own hotels, generally across the end of the platforms. Typical was the 1867 French Renaissance-style Cannon Street Hotel, a victim of World War II bombing.*

GREAT EASTERN HOTEL, LIVERPOOL STREET STATION, LONDON, E.C.2

▲ Showing a giant lobster, rather than a view of the South Eastern Hotel in Deal, Kent, must have seemed a novel idea at the time — and it has certainly stood the test of time.

▲ The Great Eastern Hotel at Liverpool Street station was completed in 1884, with an exterior inspired by Dutch architecture. It was famous for its lavish interiors; the domed dining room is seen here in a publicity postcard.

Victoria Station & Hotel, Nottingham.

Ladore Hotel. Derwentwater

LONDON & NORTH WESTERN RAILWAY COMPANY

◄ This LNWR card promoting the Ladore Hotel in the Lake District was posted in 1906, but the postmark is Bristol, so the writer was not staying there.

▲ This moonlit view of Nottingham's Victoria station and its hotel was posted in 1904, when both station and hotel were new. The Great Central Railway had completed them in 1900.

▼ Another British Transport Hotels calendar page shows the Welcombe Hotel, Stratford-upon-Avon. Despite its historic look, it did not become an LMS railway hotel until 1931.

Midland Hotel Morecambe

RESORT DURING THE SHAKESPEARE SEASON

CENTRE FOR TOURING THE COTSWOLD COUNTRY

Welcombe Hotel
STRATFORD-UPON-AVON

▲ The most famous of all 20th-century railway hotels is the Midland at Morecambe, designed by Oliver Hill in a dramatic Art Deco style and opened by the LMS in 1930 to replace the original one built in 1848. After years of neglect, it has been fully restored.

G.E.R. Hotel and Harbour, Harwich

▶ The grand Great Eastern Hotel at Harwich was opened in 1865, right on the quay, to serve the company's Continental steamers. After the GER developed a new port complex at Parkeston, the hotel declined, closing in 1922. It later became the town hall for a while.

▼ This Edwardian promotional card features the delights of the GER's Sandringham Hotel at Hunstanton, built with the aim of turning the little seaside town into a fashionable resort.

Great Eastern Railway Co's SANDRINGHAM HOTEL. HUNSTANTON-ON-SEA.

The Cosiest Nook of the beautiful Norfolk Coast faces West.

▲ Manchester and Liverpool had sumptuous and architecturally impressive hotels, thanks to their importance in railway terms. This is the grand dining room at the Midland in Manchester.

Lime Street, Liverpool.

HOLYHEAD HOTEL. L. & N.W. RAILWAY.

▲ A Liverpool landmark is the former North Western Hotel. The Renaissance-style building, designed by Alfred Waterhouse and partly inspired by Manchester Town Hall, was opened in 1871.

RAILWAY STATION HOTEL
(G.W. APPROACH)
CARDIFF

APPOINTED HOTEL   W. J. WILLIAMS, PROPRIETOR.   TELEPHONE: 2013.

◀ Another of the many independent railway hotels was in Cardiff. Its name, and the directions 'GW approach', implied a GWR connection that did not actually exist.

▲ The Holyhead Hotel, built by the Chester & Holyhead Railway in 1880, looked, until demolition in 1978, rather forbidding, but it boasted great comfort and hot and cold seawater baths.

GLASGOW &
SOUTH WESTERN RAILWAY
HOTELS

J.N.Thomas, Manager

Telegraphic Address, "SOUWESTERN".

St Enoch Station Hotel, Glasgow.

Station Hotel, Ayr.

Station Hotel, Dumfries.

Station Hotel, Turnberry, (Ayrshire).

◀ *The Glasgow & South Western Railway was an ambitious hotel owner, keen to exploit both tourism and golf. This card was sent from Ayr, one of the four destinations illustrated.*

L.M.S. HOTELS

STATION HOTEL
INVERNESS

Telephone
267
Inverness

Telegrams
Station Hotel
Inverness

AN EXTRA CHARGE FOR APARTMENTS IS MADE
IF NO MEALS ARE TAKEN IN THE HOTEL

ONE OF THE LMS HOTELS

ROOM NO. 89

PRICE

For special conditions, see inside

ARTHUR TOWLE   *Controller*   LMS HOTEL SERVICES

O.C.S.

L M S Hotel Services,
The Manageress,
Refreshment Room,
STIRLING.
LMS 74

BY   TRAIN   195

▼ *Opened in 1924 as the Caledonian Railway's greatest hotel, Gleneagles was a vast enterprise, famous for comfort, golf and tennis, as this 1950s calendar page indicates.*

FORTWILLIAM

Station Hotel, Fort William.

Aug 8th 05-

RELIABLE SERIES

◀ *Scotland was very well equipped with railway hotels, though not all were railway-owned. The West Highland Railway reached Fort William in 1894, and the hotel, seen here in 1905, soon followed.*

GOLF (KING'S AND QUEEN'S CHAMPIONSHIP COURSES) • SWIMMING

TENNIS • RIVER AND LOCH FISHING • BOWLS • CROQUET • SQUASH

Gleneagles Hotel
PERTHSHIRE

▶ *Edinburgh boasted two great rival railway hotels, the North British and the Caledonian. The latter opened in 1903, an elaborate colonnaded structure with this grand staircase at its heart.*

CALEDONIAN
RAILWAY
PRINCES ST.
STATION
HOTEL,
EDINBURGH.

GRAND
STAIRCASE.

Bedford Lemere & Co., Photographers, London.

McCorquodale & Co. Ltd., Glasgow & London.

ALONG MAIN LINES
SOUTHWEST ENGLAND

THE AMERICAN BOAT EXPRESS

BOURNEMOUTH EXPRESS, L.&S.W.R.

TRAIN SCENES

The West of England has always been a favourite region for railway photographers, offering as it does a particular combination of interesting landscapes and classic trains and locomotives. The railway has made a notable contribution, not only in terms of engineering but also through its great development of the area as a centre for leisure and holidays. Several companies played their part, but inevitably the emphasis is predominantly on the GWR.

←A smart-looking GWR Castle Class locomotive, No. 5004, 'Llanstephan Castle', stands in the sun at Bath Spa in 1948, at the head of the Bristol-bound Merchant Venturer, while the driver waits for the guard to give the 'right away'.

↓In dramatic evening light in November 1958, a pair of GWR Halls take the Plymouth train out of Newton Abbot. Ahead is the challenge of Dainton Bank, and both drivers are working their locomotives hard to build up speed. It is an image that perfectly captures the excitement of the steam age.

⬆Many West Country photographs feature Brunel's Royal Albert Bridge at Saltash. Here, with the road bridge beyond, it forms the background as a Sunday parcels train follows the Tamar headed by GWR Grange Class, No. 6824, 'Ashley Grange', in April 1962.

⬇Hayle's railway history goes back to the 1830s, when lines were built to transport copper to the docks. It was isolated until 1852, when the West Cornwall Railway linked the town to the local network. The GWR took over in 1876. Here, in the 1950s, a Penzance-bound express crosses the curving viaduct that skirts the town and harbour.

↑Double-heading was common in the West Country because of the many gradients. Here, in 1956, two GWR locomotives, Manor Class No. 7814, 'Fringford Manor' and Modified Hall Class No. 7909, 'Heveningham Hall', work hard together as they approach Hemerdon Bank, near Plympton.

↘More GWR double-heading, but this time the pairing is Hall Class No. 5940, 'Whitbourne Hall' and Castle Class No. 5056, 'Earl of Powis'. Their westbound holiday train passes the Kingsbridge branch junction at Brent in August 1956.

←The turntable at Kingswear was always a popular spot with photographers, because of the variety of locomotives to be seen using it against the backdrop of the river Dart. In September 1953 Manor Class No. 7805, 'Broome Manor', was being turned, with two other GWR Manors at work in the background.

↑The Somerset & Dorset line was also much photographed, notably by the camera of railway photographer Ivo Peters. On an early September morning in 1963 a powerful Stanier LMS locomotive, Class 8F No. 48737, hauls an interestingly mixed train towards Midsomer Norton.

↓In December 1965 the end of steam on the Southern Region is only months away, but classic scenes are still to be found. In fading light, a Merchant Navy Class Pacific, No. 35022, 'Holland–America Line', approaches Brockenhurst on the way from Bournemouth to Waterloo.

An early Class 47 diesel, still in BR two-tone green livery, hauls a long line of Midland Region carriages through the curving approach to Bristol Temple Meads. It is around 1964, and the sidings and goods yard are full of box vans and parcels carriages – a reminder of the thriving rail freight business soon to be lost.

The local photographers and enthusiasts have been rewarded by the sight of a diesel locomotive assisting a steam-hauled express up Bincombe Bank on the climb out of Weymouth. Upwey and Broadwey station is looking rather overgrown on a dull day in April 1967.

⬆ A West Country favourite was the Class 52 diesel, partly because it maintained the traditional individuality of the GWR. This is D1022, 'Western Sentinel', making plenty of smoke as it rushes past Laira depot, Plymouth, with a down express in 1975.

➡⬇ These two photographs show contrasting classic scenes of Class 52 Westerns at work on West Country expresses in the early 1970s. The setting is Somerton, seen (right) in a heavy February frost, and (below) in the soft light of late autumn.

← Another distinctive West Country diesel locomotive was the Class 42, introduced from 1958 and popularly known as Warships. Here, in 1962, D843, 'Sharpshooter', brings the London-bound Royal Duchy into Newton Abbot.

↓ As can be seen here, the Class 22 diesel locomotive was a smaller version of the Class 42 Warships. Introduced from 1959, it included 58 locomotives, all of which were scrapped by the early 1970s. Seen here running light near Plymouth in 1971, D6328 was one of the last to be withdrawn.

↓ By 1967 Ashley Hill station, north of Bristol, was but a memory, though the sign in the bushes has lingered on to mark the spot. The driver of this Hymek diesel can be seen sitting comfortably in his cab, as the Cardiff-bound train speeds up the gradient.

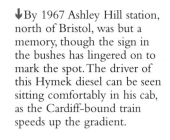

↑ By 1977 Class 50 diesels were in charge of many of the West Country expresses from Paddington. Here No. 50021, 'Rodney', passes Cowley Bridge junction on the approach to Exeter. Ten years later many Class 50s were ending their working lives on West Country expresses out of Waterloo.

↓ There were still plenty of old signs and semaphore signals to be seen around the network in the early 1970s. This is Dainton Bank, South Devon, in 1971, with a Class 47 hauling a Penzance-bound express up the steep gradient.

↑ This is another view of a Class 47, in this case hauling a Swansea-to-Paddington train up the long straight away from the Severn tunnel in September 1968. With over 500 of this successful locomotive class built since their introduction in the early 1960s, the 47s have been perennially popular with photographers all over the British railway network.

AT THE STATION

The railway network of Southwest England was created largely by the Great Western Railway and its associated companies, but the contribution made by its rival, the London & South Western Railway, should not be forgottten. For the GWR, the major hub was Bristol, the destination for Brunel's railway in the early 1840s, but many other rail centres were developed in the West Country, from Penzance to Plymouth, Exeter and Bournemouth, all linked to London by main lines. The region's cross-country routes were also important, however, and ensured an interesting variety of railway activity that would be of constant appeal to photographers.

Derry's Clock, Plymouth.

← Established in 1839, the London & South Western constantly challenged the GWR's dominance of the Southwest. Its lines spread westwards from Southampton to Exeter and Plymouth, and onwards into Cornwall. This Edwardian postcard shows the substantial LSWR offices in the centre of Plymouth. Adjacent is Derry's Clock, a feature of the town since the 1860s.

↓ Opened in 1885, Bournemouth station is a fitting reflection of the LSWR's ambitions. This grand glazed train shed, designed by W Jacomb, is still one of the most distinctive in Britain. This 1955 view shows a Portsmouth train about to depart, headed by an elderly Southern Railway Class L1 locomotive, No. 31777, with a tender still in Southern livery.

⬆ This summer 1960 view shows a busy scene at Truro. In the foreground, the local for the branch to Falmouth departs in the care of a GWR Prairie tank locomotive, No. 5537, while to the left a double-headed diesel prepares to leave for Penzance.

⬇ Penzance station, built by the Cornwall Railway in 1852, was much improved and enlarged by the GWR from 1879. It enjoys a wonderful setting by the harbour, with views over Mount's Bay. There is plenty of activity in this early 1970s view. Today it is a quieter place and a car park has been built over the lines on the left.

↓This magnificent 1960s panoramic view shows a Birmingham-to-Paignton express departing from Bristol Temple Meads, headed by one of the D600 Warship Class of diesel-hydraulic locomotives. The train is passing under the Bath Road bridge, and in the distance the curving tracks reveal the station's development from the original terminus designed by Brunel and opened in 1840.

← In April 1960 a GWR Class 4300 locomotive, No. 6384, eases its train out of Bristol Temple Meads. This locomotive was originally a Churchward design, dating back to 1911. Piles of mailbags and the water tower add period detail.

↓ The sharp curves of Bristol Temple Meads are apparent in this February 1968 photograph. Conversations continue while the Plymouth-to-Liverpool train draws into the platform, headed by a Class 52 Western diesel.

⬆It is a wet day at Barnstaple Junction and the platform is deserted. This was in fact a busy station, opened originally by the North Devon Railway in 1854 and later an important gateway to the LSWR's North Devon network, with lines going left towards Bideford and right to Ilfracombe.

⬆A typical double-headed holiday special pulls into Evercreech Junction, on the famous Somerset & Dorset route south from Bath Green Park. For decades this was a heavily worked cross-country route, famous for its locomotive diversity. It is a very different scene today, although the station building survives.

➡The GWR reached Frome in 1850, bringing a new lease of life to a quiet country town. The station, following a Brunel design, featured a timber barn-style train shed, which, remarkably, is still there. Frome was an important mainline station until 1933, when it was bypassed.

⬇Taunton station's long history goes back to 1842, when it was opened by the Bristol & Exeter Railway. Later additions have altered the original sense of classical simplicity but have added a feeling of openness. In July 2010 a London-bound First Great Western 125 waits to depart from platform 5, while a local DMU sits in the bay.

↑ A random but symmetrical group of passengers wait on the platform at Exeter St David's on a summer's day in 2010. It is a quiet moment between trains arriving and departing, with time to relax and enjoy the spaciousness of this grand station. It was opened in 1864, replacing a basic Brunel one of 1844, but the best features reflect the 1930s rebuilding by the GWR.

↑ In a scene that is an integral part of 21st-century railway station life, a woman seated on a 1950s British Railways bench makes a phone call while waiting for her train.

→ With doors open, a London-bound First Great Western 125 sits in platform 5 at Exeter St David's. Two men stand and wait, ready to wave to departing friends, but not much else is going on.

FAMOUS PLACES

DAWLISH WARREN

One of the most famous stretches of railway in southern England, and probably the most photographed, is the line westwards from Exeter to Newton Abbot, much of which is on an embankment built right along the seashore. Cuttings and tunnels add to the excitement. The route, engineered by Brunel and opened in 1846, was operated briefly and unsuccessfully by his atmospheric system. A conventional railway since 1848, the line has been famous for the quantity and diversity of its traffic, much augmented by the development of the South Devon holiday resorts. Since the closures of the 1960s, the line, which requires constant maintenance and has on occasion been broken by the sea, has carried all trains serving Plymouth and beyond.

← Many postcards depict the scenic qualities of the line, and this Edwardian example is typical. Perhaps the waves breaking over the embankment ahead of the train might seem like artistic licence, but this has always been quite a common occurrence.

→ Another, more recent postcard shows very clearly how the winding line follows the shore, separating the beaches from the adjacent towns and villages.

2 7094 DAWLISH FROM LANGSTONE CLIFF, DAWLISH WARREN.

↗ In the late summer of 1959 the Devonian, hauled by Castle Class locomotive No. 4077, 'Chepstow Castle', sets off for Exeter and London, while the driver watches the signals. The long train, typical of that era, is full of returning holidaymakers.

↑Holidaymakers, mainly men, line up to watch another Castle Class locomotive as it hauls its train towards Teignmouth in August 1962. In the last years of GWR steam, the Dawlish route was a trainspotter's dream.

↑A calm sea laps at the edge of the embankment as the Cornish Riviera Express heads eastwards, drawn by one of the distinctive Western Region Warship diesels, a short-lived class in service between 1960 and 1971.

↘In the 1980s the route became the province of the HST 125s. In August 1981, this London-bound HST set races past the remains of Starcross pumping house, one of the few relics of Brunel's atmospheric railway.

↗With Dawlish in the background and a few figures on the beach on a mild day in August 1998, a Class 47 locomotive, No. 47814, hauls its Virgin-liveried train away from the station.

TUNNELS, BRIDGES & VIADUCTS

Many companies were involved in building the railways of the West Country, but the key figure is undoubtedly Isambard Kingdom Brunel. His Great Western Railway was a revolutionary enterprise, built at a huge cost to fulfil the demands of his broad-gauge dream, and his legacy includes a series of spectacular viaducts and tunnels built to overcome the challenging landscape. The tunnels are impressive, but the viaducts are spectacular, with 48 on the main line between Newton Abbot and Penzance, all originally built in timber.

↑Brunel was an accomplished architect as well as a great engineer, and he used both Gothic and Classical styles for his tunnels. This is the castellated portal for Twerton, on the outskirts of Bath, seen in 1956 on a summer's evening as GWR King Class, No. 6003, 'King George IV', effortlessly hauls a Bristol-bound train out of the tunnel. The driver, looking relaxed, watches the photographer.

➜Another castellated Brunel tunnel is Bristol No. 2, by St Anne's Park. With a light covering of snow on the ground, the down Bristol Pullman exits the tunnel during the winter of 1968. The Blue Pullmans were the last phase of a long and distinguished history of scheduled luxury mainline travel; the Western Region ones, to Bristol and Cardiff, were phased out in 1973.

⬆ St Pinnock viaduct in the Glynn valley is, at 151ft, the highest on the GWR's West Country route. The original timber structure was replaced in the 1880s with wrought-iron girders built onto the raised stone piers visible in this 1955 photograph. In 1964 the track was singled, following concerns about excess weight damaging the viaduct. Here, trains for Exeter and Penzance are about to pass. The locomotives are No. 5003 (Exeter train) and No. 6873.

Saltash Passage

⬆ The last of Brunel's timber viaducts to remain in use was College Wood, on the Falmouth branch. It survived until 1934, when it was finally replaced. The original piers stand alongside the new arches.

⬅ Brunel's greatest railway structure, and one of the best in Britain, is his Royal Albert Bridge, carrying the GWR high above the Tamar at Saltash. Visually exciting and revolutionary in its engineering, it was opened in 1859. This card also shows the ferry.

GOODS TRAINS

In the past, the railway network of Southwest England was famous for its rural routes and branch lines, many of which were lost during the 1960s. Until that time, country areas were dependent on the railway for their supplies and for the distribution of agricultural produce. Much of the goods traffic was, therefore, quite local, but important nationally was the transport of minerals, primarily clay and stone, along with oil and fertilizers. Some of this traffic survives today.

←On a sunny day in the 1960s, a Beattie well tank shunts clay wagons at Wenford Bridge, the terminus of a remote rural branch line near Bodmin, in Cornwall. The local nature of this scene is misleading, for these clay wagons are destined for long journeys to industrial centres.

INSERT DETAILS IN BLOCK LETTERS
BRITISH RAILWAYS
(WESTERN REGION)
Loaded Time
999-7-0

LIVE STOCK

No. and Description of Animals
Watered
And/or Time
Fed at Date
Required to be Milked Time
Not later than Date
Time
Charge To pay £

TO

VIA Region Section

Owner and No. of Wagon

3

Sheets in or on Wagon

Name & Address of Consignee

Sender

↓As the evening light throws shadows across Brunel's Royal Albert Bridge, a GWR Class 6800 locomotive, No. 6824, 'Ashley Grange', hauls a mixed freight westwards into Cornwall. This evocative image was a common sight in 1962, but all was soon to change.

↑ The transport of coal was a continuous process. In 1960 a Class 7200 tank locomotive hauls a coal train past Upton Scudamore, near Warminster. This class of 2-8-2 heavy goods locomotives was introduced by the GWR in 1934 primarily for the coal trade.

↑ This 1960s photograph shows a GWR tank locomotive, No. 4658, hustling its train of loaded coal wagons alongside the sea near Teignmouth, while an Exeter-bound express disappears into the distance.

↖ It is near the end of steam on the Southern Region, and the last steam-hauled freight to leave Weymouth is tackling the notorious Bincombe Bank, a few miles north. Headed by an unidentified West Country Class locomotive, it has the usual banker at the rear.

← The distinctive Western Region Class 52 diesel locomotives were normally seen in more favourable circumstances. Here, a dirty-looking No. 1058, 'Western Nobleman', soon to be scrapped, is still earning its keep hauling a loaded stone train near Westbury, Wiltshire, in June 1976.

LOCOMOTIVE SHEDS

The Southwest's particular combination of main lines, rural routes and branch lines required a large number of sheds, the majority of which were quite small. The region's major sheds – Eastleigh, Bristol, Exmouth Junction and Newton Abbot – all controlled a huge area. Newton Abbot's, for example, extended to Penzance. The legacy of ancient inter-company rivalries, maintained even during the British Railways era, meant that there was considerable duplication, with places such as Yeovil and Bath still having two sheds.

A number of small subsidiary sheds served the complicated network of the old LSWR's north Cornwall route. This is Wadebridge in the 1930s, with an old shed by then too small for the locomotives in its care.

Laira has a long history, going back to the 1840s, but from 1901 it became an important steam shed. Unlike many sheds, it survived the transition from steam to diesel, and was in fact expanded and rebuilt to cater for new diesels, notably the Westerns, three of which are lined up here in this 1960s photograph.

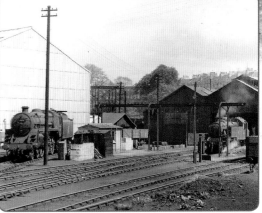

⬆ Templecombe, the meeting point for the Waterloo-to-Exeter main line and the Somerset & Dorset Joint Railway, was an exciting place for enthusiasts because of the rich mix of GWR, SR and BR Standard locomotives to be seen. Here, in the early 1960s, SR U Class No. 31632 is turned.

➡ Traffic demands and old GWR/LMS rivalries ensured that Bath had two sheds. Shown here near the end of its life is the one that served the old Somerset & Dorset line, with a British Railways Standard Class 5 locomotive waiting for duty.

⬇ The size of the shed at Exmouth junction reflected its status as a primary shed with more than twelve subsidiaries, stretching from Salisbury to Bude. It is seen here in SR days.

RAILWAY WORKS

There were several locations in the West of England where railway vehicles were built, but all were overshadowed by Swindon. In 1841 IK Brunel and Daniel Gooch recommended to their directors that the Great Western Railway's works be built at this small and remote Wiltshire village. Intended initially as a repair workshop, the Swindon works opened in 1843, but soon began to build locomotives, establishing a tradition that was to be maintained until the 1970s. The GWR built not only a huge works complex, one of the best in Britain, but also a railway town, complete with shops, churches, schools and medical facilities. The works was closed in 1986, but some buildings and, of course, the town, live on.

← From small beginnings in the 1840s Swindon grew rapidly, becoming one of the largest railway works in Britain. Carriages were first built in 1868, and expansion was continuous, especially after the end of the broad gauge. By 1914 the works covered over 300 acres and employed 12,000 people.

↓ All aspects of railway vehicle construction were undertaken, with many specialist workshops including foundries, wheels, tenders, carpentry, upholstery and painting. There was a large design office and a sequence of famous chief mechanical engineers: Gooch, Armstrong, Dean, Churchward, Collett and Hawksworth.

←→ From its early days, Swindon opened its doors to visitors, a tradition maintained into the British Railways era. This 1960 visitors' guide shows both steam and diesel locomotives under construction. The map reveals the scale and complexity of the site.

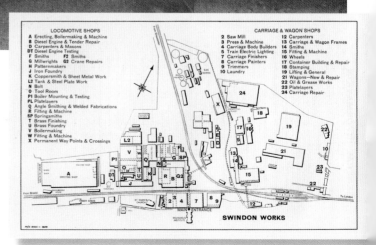

LOCOMOTIVE SHOPS

A Erecting, Boilermaking & Machine
B Diesel Engine & Tender Repair
C Carpenters & Masons
DT Diesel Engine Testing
F Smiths   F2 Smiths
G Millwrights G2 Crane Repairs
H Patternmakers
J Iron Foundry
K Coppersmith & Sheet Metal Work
L2 Tank & Steel Plate Work
N Bolt
O Tool Room
P1 Boiler Mounting & Testing
PL Platelayers
Q Angle Smithing & Welded Fabrications
R Fitting & Machine
SP Springsmiths
T Brass Finishing
U Brass Foundry
V Boilermaking
W Fitting & Machine
X Permanent Way Points & Crossings

CARRIAGE & WAGON SHOPS

2 Saw Mill
3 Press & Machine
4 Carriage Body Builders
5 Train Electric Lighting
7 Carriage Finishers
8 Carriage Painters
9 Trimmers
10 Laundry
12 Carpenters
13 Carriage & Wagon Frames
14 Smiths
15 Fitting & Machine
16 Wheels
17 Container Building & Repair
18 Stamping
19 Lifting & General
21 Wagons—New & Repair
22 Oil & Grease Works
23 Platelayers
24 Carriage Repair

SWINDON WORKS

↘Swindon had several workshops devoted to the construction and mounting of boilers, as well as several erecting shops equipped with large overhead cranes capable of lifting up to 100 tons. There were also extensive repair and maintenance facilities.

➔Another West Country works was that built in the early 1860s at Highbridge for the Somerset & Dorset Joint Railway. This was a much smaller enterprise, but locomotives and rolling stock were built there until 1929. This card shows the war memorial at the works, erected to commemorate employees killed in World War I.

⬇Locomotive construction continued at Swindon well into the diesel era, with several famous classes being built there. Notable were the distinctive Westerns and Warships, which maintained the spirit of GWR individuality into the modern age. Here, in 1963, three Westerns are in for repair.

ALONG MAIN LINES
SOUTHERN ENGLAND

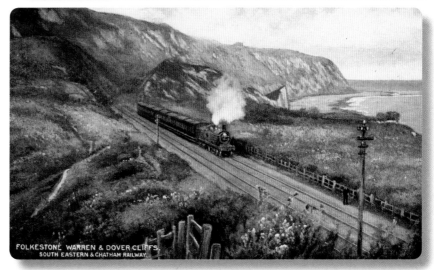

FOLKESTONE WARREN & DOVER CLIFFS.
SOUTH EASTERN & CHATHAM RAILWAY.

TRAIN SCENES

The railway network of southern England has always been dominated by the necessary operation of commuter services, and these have tended to overshadow the many mainline expresses that either ran within the region or passed through it on their routes from London. Many of these routes are still there, with fast and efficient services, but today they are operated by standard modern trains that lack the glamour of the steam age. Then, named trains served the Kent and Sussex coast, the Channel ports and the West Country. Even the ordinary service and commuter trains of that period seem more interesting than their modern-day equivalents.

←On a clear summer's day a Standard Class 4 locomotive, No. 75065, fills the sky with smoke and steam as it drags the heavy Ramsgate train out of Victoria station and up the steep Grosvenor Bank. Introduced from 1951, and designed and built in Derby, Brighton, Swindon, Crewe and Doncaster, the Standard classes were part of British Railways' new look.

↓Another Standard classic, Britannia or 7MT Class No. 70004, 'William Shakespeare', hauls the Golden Arrow through north Kent in July 1955 on the first leg of this most famous international Pullman service. Britannias were often used for this prestige service, always immaculately turned out.

↑Rebuilt Merchant Navy class Pacifics were a familiar sight on West Country expresses to and from Waterloo, so this might well be No. 35008, 'Orient Line', on a normal day's work. In fact, it is 2 July 1967, the final day of steam on the Southern Region, and the locomotive is hauling a special back to Waterloo for the last time.

↑Another popular Pullman service was the Brighton Belle, which operated initially as the Southern Belle. From 1933 until the final run in the early 1970s, it was uniquely an all–Pullman electric train, famously completing the journey in an hour.

←During the summer of 1949 a streamlined, or 'air-smoothed', West Country Class locomotive, No. 34011, 'Tavistock', waits at Exmouth junction to take the Devon Belle back to Waterloo. This luxury Pullman train, introduced in 1947, ran from London to Plymouth and Ilfracombe.

⬆This British Railways postcard was issued to promote the Kentish Belle, a Pullman service to Ramsgate. Starting life in 1948 as the Thanet Belle, it was renamed in 1951 and continued to run until 1958, when electrification of the route brought it to an end.

⬆Another rebuilt West Country Pacific, No. 34025, 'Whimple', hauls a service train through the hills at Folkestone Warren. By now this locomotive, like so many Bulleid Pacifics, had seen better days. Dirty and unkempt, it was spending its final years on minor duties.

⬇The South Eastern Railway turned Folkestone from a small fishing harbour into a major cross-Channel port. The short branch that linked the harbour and the main line at Folkestone Junction was steeply graded, and and trains had to be banked. Here, in the 1950s, tank locomotives struggle to haul a heavy boat train up the gradient.

➡Until the advent of Eurostar, the Night Ferry was Britain's only truly international train. Introduced in 1936, it was an overnight through service between London and Paris and, from 1956, Brussels. The train of Continental Wagon-Lits sleepers crossed the Channel on a train ferry. The service ended in 1980.

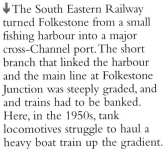

On lesser routes, such as the cross-country line from Redhill to Tonbridge, regular service trains were often hauled by elderly locomotives in semi-retirement. In June 1960, a Wainwright-designed 4-4-0 L Class locomotive, No. 31778, of World War I vintage, was on duty.

In the summer of 1959, steam surrounds a Southern Railway N15 Class locomotive, No. 30804, as it takes its Ramsgate-bound train through Bromley South. A pair of Pullmans suggest it may be a legacy of the Kentish Belle, which had ceased running the previous year.

← A Class V locomotive, No. 30909, a Maunsell 1930s design, with a rake of red-liveried coaches, drifts through the countryside near Wadhurst, between Tunbridge Wells and Robertsbridge, in 1957. Commonplace scenes like this represented the real life of the railways in that era.

↓ One of the most unusual locomotives designed by Bulleid for the Southern Railway was the Austerity Q1 of 1942. Here, No. 33027 and another class member are on duty with a Locomotive Club of Great Britain rail tour at Baynards station just before the Cranleigh line closed in 1965.

↓ Another elderly Southern Railway 4-4-0 earns its keep taking a heavy holiday train out of Margate in the late 1950s. The track has been electrified, so the steam age is about to end on this famous route.

⬆A notable railway location in Hampshire was Shawford, where the GWR line from Didcot to Winchester Chesil via Newbury joined the main line to Southampton. Here, in 1957, the famous locomotive 'City of Truro' is seen on regular duties, with a Didcot-to-Southampton service.

⬊London is the railway hub of southern England, the starting point for journeys to every corner of Britain. In May 1963, the great LNER classic, Class A4 No. 60007, 'Sir Nigel Gresley', makes a smoky exit from Gasworks tunnel, setting off northwards from Kings Cross with the White Rose.

LONDON STATIONS

Euston, London's first terminus station, opened in 1838. Others quickly followed, reflecting the ambitions of the many Victorian railway companies keen to serve the capital. This process continued until 1899, when the Great Central Railway finally completed its costly route with the opening of Marylebone. By then there were 17 terminus stations in London, ranged roughly in a circle around the city. With the exception of Waterloo and London Bridge, all were north of the Thames. Since then only Broad Street and Holborn Viaduct have been lost, while others have changed in status. The major change in recent years has been the opening of international stations, first at Waterloo and then at St Pancras.

← Euston expanded steadily from the 1830s on, and by the end of the Victorian era had become a dark, confusing labyrinth. This 1913 card, issued by the LNWR for promotional purposes, shows the Irish Mail ready to depart.

↓ Rebuilding plans by the LMS were brought to a halt by World War II, so the old Euston lingered on. Here, in July 1953, the Royal Scot has arrived, double-headed by two old LMS stalwarts, a 1920s 4-4-0 and a later Jubilee.

← Euston's ancient and gloomy nature is obvious in this official British Railways photograph showing passengers sitting by the arrivals indicator in 1950.

←This 1907 postcard shows Liverpool Street's original entrance, in all its neo-Gothic glory. Designed by Edward Wilson and completed in 1874, the station became increasingly chaotic once it started to expand in the 1880s.

↖The great sweep of Euston's original glazed train shed, covering 15 platforms, is revealed in this photograph taken by British Railways shortly before the complete demolition and rebuilding that took place in the 1960s.

↓Marylebone, London's most recent station, opened in 1899. Small and decorative, it has been well restored. The porte cochère leads to the hotel.

↑This LNER era Class N7 tank engine, a design built progressively from the 1920s, rests between platforms at Liverpool Street in the 1950s, awaiting either the station pilot or carriage-shunting duties.

↑St Pancras changed little over the decades, though various attempts were made to brighten its aspect. This shows one attempt: the installation of timetable and advertising boards in 1951.

↓There are a number of postcard views of St Pancras. This colourful and busy Edwardian example is entitled: 'Going North for the Holidays. Midland Railway'.

↑After years of neglect, restoration work on Gilbert Scott's magnificent and wildly extravagant Grand Midland Hotel of 1876 began in the 1990s, prior to the opening of the St Pancras international station. It reopened as a hotel in May 2011.

↓The splendid facade of St Pancras conceals an even greater wonder: Barlow's vast iron and glass train shed of 1868, seen here in the 1980s. At 243ft wide and 110ft high, it was for years the largest unsupported span in the world.

↑As a casually dressed porter wanders past a line of empty parcel trolleys, an LNER Class A3, No. 60044, 'Melton', waits to depart from Kings Cross in the 1950s.

↓An impressive diesel line-up at Kings Cross in August 1978 features alternating Class 47s and Class 55 Deltics.

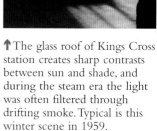

↑The glass roof of Kings Cross station creates sharp contrasts between sun and shade, and during the steam era the light was often filtered through drifting smoke. Typical is this winter scene in 1959.

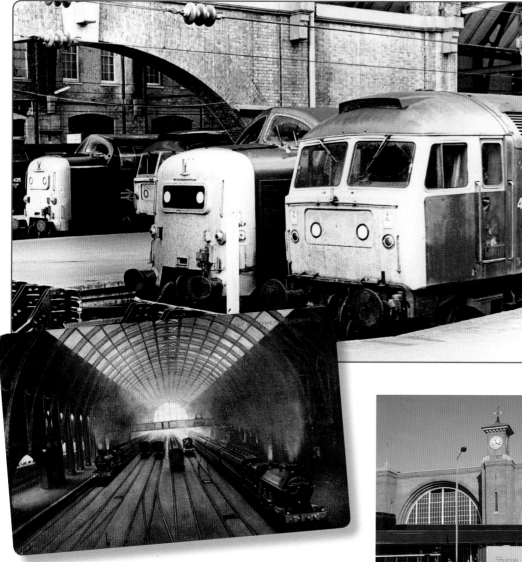

↓The functional, symmetrical yet elegant architecture of Kings Cross, with its arrival and departure bays, has long been highly regarded, even though it was always an operationally difficult station. Here, in the 1980s, forecourt clutter greatly diminished the building's visual impact.

↑This Edwardian card of the old arrival platforms at Kings Cross during the days of the GNR wonderfully illustrates the particular quality and style of the station.

←Paddington's 1830s station was a temporary timber structure, eventually replaced by the great 1850s cathedral-like iron and glass train shed designed by Brunel and Digby Wyatt. It is fronted by a passenger concourse, seen here with the buffer screen of 1958.

↓This Edwardian postcard reveals the magnificence of Paddington's original train shed, quite uncompromised by later additions to the north and to the south.

↗It is 9.45am in August 1943 and Paddington is partially blacked out. Platform One is crowded with passengers, a few in uniform. More servicemen can be seen on the train about to depart.

↑Opened in 1864 at the northern end of Hungerford Bridge, Charing Cross allowed the South Eastern Railway to claim that its trains served London's West End. In 1958 SR Schools Class locomotive No. 30937, 'Epsom', waits under the 1905 roof.

←In 1990 an office complex designed by Terry Farrell (also shown on page 109) was built over Charing Cross.

↑With the completion of Cannon Street in 1866, the SER was able to deliver its passengers to the heart of the City of London. This early 20th-century postcard shows Sir John Hawkshaw's original train shed.

←The remains of Cannon Street's train shed, severely damaged by bombing in World War II, were still standing in 1956. Today, only the towers remain, and offices have been built over the station.

↑↗ Waterloo opened in 1848. Its subsequent piecemeal development was unplanned and chaotic, and between 1900 and 1921 it was completely rebuilt by the LSWR, becoming one of London's best looking and most efficient mainline stations.

↓ Until 1924 Victoria was two stations. Adjoining but unconnected, they were built in 1860 and 1862 by different railway companies. Both were rebuilt in distinctly separate but equally grand styles in the Edwardian era, with plenty of sculptural decoration.

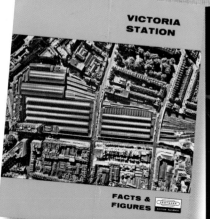

↑ The redevelopment of St Pancras as an international station and the London terminus for high-speed trains arriving via the Channel Tunnel was a spectacular achievement, successfully blending the exciting qualities of the Victorian building with dynamic modern architecture. Eurostar trains now enter and leave beneath ironwork painted in sky blue, the train shed's original colour.

→ The station's former vaults, built mostly for the handling and storage of beer barrels and other Midland Railway freight, have been turned into a vast passenger concourse, with shops, cafés and the international departure hall.

↓ Unlike its neighbour, Kings Cross is largely recognizable as Cubitt's Victorian station. In 2010 two East Coast HST 125s wait to depart.

↙ Since the mindless and largely unnecessary destruction of Euston in the early 1960s, London's Victorian stations have generally been treated with care and consideration. A good example, seen here, is Liverpool Street, which was redeveloped during the 1980s.

→ Waterloo's splendid concourse has seen many changes, but the inherent quality of the architectural space is still apparent as it absorbs the modern retail environment with ease.

↓ Apart from bomb damage in 1941, Paddington remains much as the late Victorians would have known it. It is still a richly impressive station, revealing the original vision of Brunel and Digby Wyatt. Even the electric Heathrow Express in the foreground barely affects the architecture.

⬆ Terry Farrell's office development dwarfs Charing Cross station and has made the platforms a bit gloomy. However, it is an exciting echo of the station's original iron train shed, which collapsed in 1905, and it has retained the Southern Railway's 1930s branding.

⬆ Stations are adaptable spaces, able to reflect changes in traffic patterns and social behaviour. The challenge is to balance the qualities of the old with the needs of the new. Ticket gates and colourful South West trains fit well into Waterloo's grandeur.

FAMOUS PLACES

CLAPHAM JUNCTION

Clapham Junction, in Battersea, is a confusion dating back to 1863. It was built as an interchange station by the London & South Western and the London, Brighton & South Coast railways where their routes converged. Originally the two companies had separate entrances, but regular redevelopment has changed this, though the LB&SC's imposing 1910 building survives, albeit not in railway use. Clapham Junction has long claimed to be Europe's busiest station, and today about 2,000 trains pass through each day, most of which stop. There are also connections to the Midlands, the North and the West Country.

↑Elegantly posed with a careful symmetry, this group of LB&SC station staff was photographed in about 1900. The positions the men are in, and the variations in their uniform, define their status.

↑This Edwardian postcard shows the northern side of Clapham Junction with an LSWR train in the platform and goods wagons, also part of the interchange process, in the foreground.

↓A British Railways Standard Class 5 locomotive races through Clapham Junction in the mid-1960s. The poster alongside the line shows the way to the future.

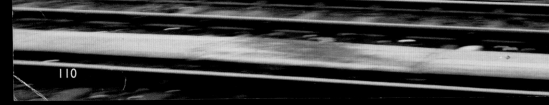

↓In 1985 a smart-looking Class 33 diesel, No. 33032, draws its train into the station. Popularly known as Cromptons, this large class was introduced in 1957, primarily for use on the Southern Region.

↑This illustration from a 1950s children's book gives an idea of the scale and complexity of the track, and the variety of the traffic, at Clapham Junction. The chimneys of Battersea power station stand on the horizon.

↗A Waterloo-to-Reading train, with a Victorian locomotive heading an equally elderly collection of carriages, passes beneath the famous elevated signal box at Clapham Junction in July 1926.

→On a sunny January day in 2001 the Gatwick Express, its brand new stock resplendent in a new livery, sweeps through the station on its non-stop journey to the airport. The name board still proclaims Clapham Junction to be 'Britain's Busiest Railway Station'.

Welcome to Clapham Junction
Britain's busiest railway station

TUNNELS, BRIDGES & VIADUCTS

The developed nature, established road patterns and varied landscape of southern England, with its hills and river valleys, presented many challenges to the early railway builders, resulting in some dramatic examples of tunnels and viaducts. Later, the density of the expanding commuter network and the steady increase in traffic created new engineering demands. The major structures were on the main lines, but lesser lines were not without features of engineering interest. Some, inevitably, were lost after the widespread closures of the 1960s.

➡ In order to reach the port of Dover from Folkestone, William Cubitt, the South Eastern Railway's engineer, took the line along the coast. This required three tunnels, the longest and most dramatic of which was a twin bore through Shakespeare Cliff. Completed in 1844, it opened directly onto the beach, the track then being carried along the shore on a trestle. This 1920s image, although its focus is on the lady, shows it well.

⬇ This postcard view shows the distinctive tall, arched portals at the eastern end of the Shakespeare Cliff tunnel, with an SER Dover express emerging. Posted in 1906 from central London to Haslemere, the message, as so often, has nothing to do with trains.

➘ At Worting junction, west of Basingstoke, the LSWR's two main lines, to Weymouth and to Exeter and the West Country, diverge. Traffic demands required the building of a flyover, the Battledown viaduct, seen here in an early 20th-century view.

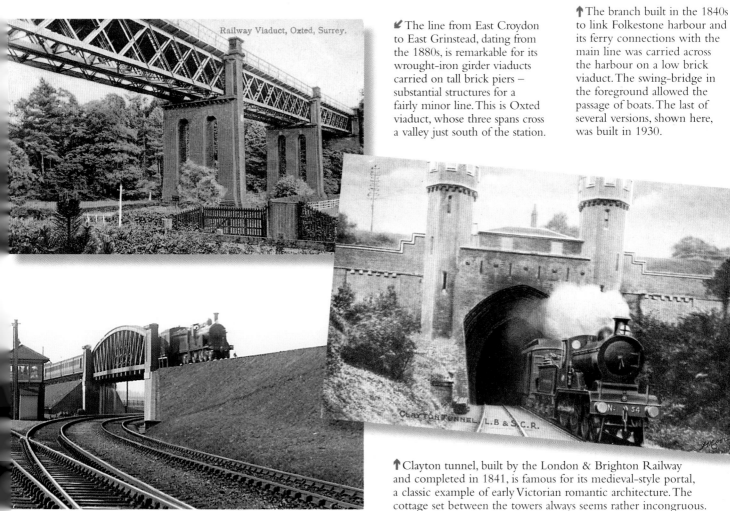

The line from East Croydon to East Grinstead, dating from the 1880s, is remarkable for its wrought-iron girder viaducts carried on tall brick piers – substantial structures for a fairly minor line. This is Oxted viaduct, whose three spans cross a valley just south of the station.

Railway Viaduct, Oxted, Surrey.

The branch built in the 1840s to link Folkestone harbour and its ferry connections with the main line was carried across the harbour on a low brick viaduct. The swing-bridge in the foreground allowed the passage of boats. The last of several versions, shown here, was built in 1930.

Clayton tunnel, built by the London & Brighton Railway and completed in 1841, is famous for its medieval-style portal, a classic example of early Victorian romantic architecture. The cottage set between the towers always seems rather incongruous.

GOODS TRAINS

Commuter and suburban lines dominate the network in the South of England, with seemingly little room for freight services. Yet these have always been an important part of the infrastructure, carrying local supplies and produce and handling much of Britain's international traffic via the Channel ports. All this required large marshalling yards of the kind shown in the photograph below. There were also regular trains serving the oil terminals and refineries, and carrying bulk cargoes such as cement and coal. Today, the marshalling yards have gone, but the container terminals keep the freight running.

→ In the 1950s, an elderly Class S15 locomotive, No. 30501, takes a mixed freight through Virginia Water station, on its way to Feltham yards. The S15 class was an LSWR design introduced in 1920 for mixed traffic work

↘ At Hither Green, to the southeast of London, there was a major engine shed and a huge network of marshalling yards. This 1960 photograph shows a general view, along with the specialized depot for handling perishable cargoes to and from the Continent.

BRITISH RAILWAYS

REGION

B.R. 11222

FOR INTERNAL USE

This Wagon May Travel Empty
For One Journey Only

HITHER GREEN

From

To

Date   1 3 FEB 1973

Any authorised person obscuring or removing this card render himself liable to Criminal Prosecution.

→ In April 1959 an uncared-for King Arthur Class locomotive, No. 30797, draws a mixed collection of parcels vans along the main line north of Orpington, Kent. Nearing the end of its life, the locomotive has already lost its nameplate, 'Sir Blamor de Ganis'.

←With Basingstoke in the distance, a train of empty milk tankers and a couple of box vans approaches Worting junction on its way to a West Country dairy in July 1964. The locomotive, a famous member of the Battle of Britain Class, No. 34066, 'Spitfire', makes light work of the load while the fireman leans out to check the wagons.

↓Reading has always been an important station, not least because of the link line to Basingstoke, used for exchanging traffic between companies, such as GWR and LSWR, and later between British Rail's Western and Southern regions. Here, in 1964, a Class 33 diesel takes the Reading West curve with a mixed freight.

LOCOMOTIVE SHEDS

The busy networks in the South of England, dominated as they were by short-distance and commuter routes, required a large pool of locomotives and, therefore, a series of substantial sheds to service and maintain them. Many, for example Old Oak Common and Hornsey, were in and around London, serving mainline termini, while others looked after such major rail centres as Guildford or Brighton and catered for both suburban and long-distance traffic. Most railway works, including Ashford and Eastleigh, had associated sheds, with major repair facilities.

← At Hornsey in north London, lines of tank and mixed-traffic locomotives reveal the kind of work done here. It is the early 1920s, soon after the formation of the LNER, and some engines still have GNR markings.

↓ Guildford had a relatively small shed, considering the variety of work in the area. In 1963 a Victorian Class B4 tank locomotive on shed duties shunts across the turntable.

A great variety of Southern Railway locomotives sit coaled and ready for work at Brighton shed, which had to cater for express passenger, goods and local services. The date is probably the mid-1940s.

A solitary enthusiast at Ashford shed in the early 1950s has plenty of choices for his notebook, with locomotives from many classes old and new lined up. First in line is a Class O1 veteran from the Edwardian era.

This illustration from a 1950s children's book shows cleaners, possibly apprentices, at work on 'Lord Rodney', Lord Nelson Class No. 30851, on shed somewhere in southern England.

The line-up at Eastleigh shed in this 1950s photograph includes another view of 'Lord Rodney', the locomotive in the middle, flanked by two elderly Victorians, a T9 and an M7 tank.

RAILWAY WORKS

For much of the 19th century there were three major railway companies operating in southern England: the South Eastern Railway, the London, Brighton & South Coast Railway, and the London & South Western Railway. All three companies built large locomotive and carriage works, at Ashford, Brighton and Eastleigh respectively, replacing earlier but smaller works closer to London, such as Nine Elms. All survived amalgamations to become part of the Southern Railway and lived on into – and in the case of Eastleigh beyond – the British Railways era. Like Eastleigh, the town of Ashford owes its existence to the railway, having started as workers' housing on a greenfield site.

BRITISH ELECTRICAL POWER CONVENTION

VISIT TO BRIGHTON WORKS OF BRITISH RAILWAYS SOUTHERN REGION

WEDNESDAY, 20TH JUNE, 1951

↓→As elsewhere, open days and official visits were important. This brochure, produced for a 1951 visit to Brighton works, includes a map of the 9-acre site.

↓The LB&SC established its major railway works at Brighton in 1854. It quickly became the town's main industry, producing locomotives, carriages and wagons. This shows the scale of the works during the late Victorian period, with long lines of locomotives under construction. By 1947 a thousand locomotives had been built at Brighton. The works closed from 1958.

→ Having struggled for years with its Nine Elms site, the LSWR moved its carriage and wagon works to Eastleigh in 1891. A few years later locomotive building began, establishing a large works that remains operational. Here, in the 1950s, two former Southern Railway locomotives are being repaired.

↑ In 1962 a visitor to Eastleigh works photographed two 1930s Southern Railway U Class locomotives as they were undergoing a complete rebuild in what seem to be rather chaotic conditions.

→ The LB&SC opened a new carriage and wagon works at Lancing in 1912, to ease overcrowding at the Brighton site. Rapidly successful, and with a reputation for stability and quality, the works eventually employed 1,500 people. It was closed in the 1960s.

← Ashford works was opened in 1847, following the closure of the SER's New Cross site. Still important well into the British Railways era, it finally closed in 1982.

4073

© M. CLARK

10341 "The Re

ALONG MAIN LINES
WALES

L.&N.W.R. IRISH BOAT EXPRESS
Britannia Bridge, Menai Straits

720

Express

British Railways Photo

Copyright. COAL TRAIN LEAVING FOR THE DOCKS. H. Fleur

ALAN ANDERSON

1A71

TRAIN SCENES

Today, main lines in Wales are few and far between and mostly follow the north or south coasts. Everything in between is now rather quiet and rural, but it was all very different up to the 1960s, with mainline expresses crossing the country from centres such as Shrewsbury, Chester, Newport and Wrexham and linking the major towns on the west coast. Victorian rivalries between the GWR and the LNWR, and later the LMS, were maintained until the British Railways era, ensuring lively competition for business and holiday traffic. This was an exciting period for railway enthusiasts, and photographs from this time document not just the last years of steam in Wales but also the end of most of the Welsh mainline network.

↓ One of Wales's most important trains was the Cambrian Coast Express. In 1966 this was still running and is seen here descending Talerddig Bank, Powys, with a pair of unkempt British Railways Standard Class 4 locomotives in charge.

← Blasting smoke and steam, a British Railways Standard Class 4 tank locomotive, No. 80091, draws a local under Rhyl's impressive signal gantry. It is 1958, when Rhyl was still a major holiday destination.

↑ The line along the north coast of Wales, built by the Chester & Holyhead Railway, was always busy with holiday trains, freight and traffic for Ireland. In the early 1960s, this double-headed holiday express approaches Colwyn Bay.

↖Dovey Junction used to be a meeting point for mainline expresses. Here, in the early 1960s, GWR Manor Class locomotive No. 7828, 'Odney Manor', blows off steam as it approaches the junction with a train of Midland Region carriages bound for Aberystwyth.

←In 1948, when this photograph was taken, three mainline routes converged in Barmouth, making it a major centre for holiday traffic. Here, a push-pull unit headed by an elderly GWR tank locomotive rests near the carriage sidings.

↓Another British Railways Standard Class 4 locomotive, No. 75016, takes the down Cambrian Coast Express across the river Severn near Welshpool in 1966.

↓On a quiet evening in 1978 a two-car DMU waits to depart from Llandudno Junction, a major stopping point on the route to Holyhead. A branch serves Llandudno itself, still a traditional resort, set below the Great Orme.

↗In 1989 a special rail tour, celebrating 150 years of the Midland Counties Railway, races along the coast of North Wales near Penmaenmawr, headed by a red-liveried Class 47 diesel.

➡When Robert Stephenson took the railway across the river from Llandudno to Conwy, he was conscious of its castle and its history, and, where the line pierced the medieval walls, he built a Gothic arch. By 1978 many routes in Wales were operated by diesel multiple units like the one seen here passing on market day.

↘In the heyday of steam, Princess Coronation Class locomotives were rarely seen in Wales. This means that this classic view of No. 46229, 'Duchess of Hamilton', drawing its train of GWR-liveried carriages out of Stephenson's wrought-iron tubular bridge and into Conwy, with the castle immediately above, is too good to be true: it is actually a steam-hauled rail tour in July 1991.

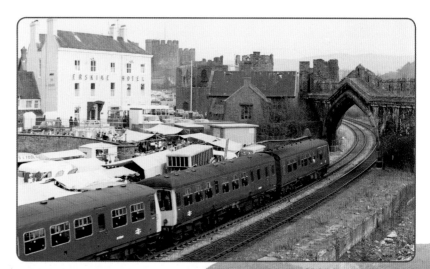

↑A pair of Class 37 diesels meet on the approach to Newport tunnels in 1987, one running light and the other in charge of an engineering train equipped for track renewal. Over 300 of these multi-purpose locomotives were built between 1960 and 1965.

↓By 1988 Wales's most important main line was the route to Swansea from Paddington, and the typical train was an HST 125 nine-car unit. This one, with mixed InterCity and British Rail liveries, is approaching its journey's end at Swansea.

AT THE STATION

Aside from the few main lines, the railway map of Wales was built in a somewhat piecemeal fashion by small, independent companies. The transport of coal or stone was the inspiration for many of them, along with the needs of local communities that were relatively inaccessible before the coming of the railways. Later in the 19th century, tourism became an important factor, with coastal and mountain resorts and spas enjoying rapid growth. The stations of Wales are, therefore, interestingly diverse, reflecting the different periods of development as well as the sense of local pride that was a driving force behind the building of many of the lines.

➜The first station in Aberystwyth was opened by the Cambrian Railway in 1864. It was an unimpressive building with no street presence. In 1924 the GWR, having taken over the Cambrian, greatly expanded the station and added the white stone frontage seen here, designed in a generic classical style, complete with clock tower. Today, the station, with much reduced traffic, has reverted to the original Cambrian building.

⬇In June 1953 coronation decorations adorn Cardiff General, another station rebuilt by the GWR, in this case in the 1930s and in a much more dynamic Art Deco style. In the centre, locomotives on the Red Dragon change, with a new-looking British Railways Standard, No. 70026, 'Polar Star', ready to take over from GWR Castle Class No. 5020, 'Trematon Castle'.

AWH. 324.

THE RAILWAY STATION, ABERYSTWYTH

Copyright Frith Ltd.

←Carmarthen, on the main line to Pembroke and Fishguard, was also a junction for the GWR's link northwards to Aberystwyth. It served a largely rural area but, as this 1920s photograph suggests, it was a substantial station. As so often in that era, everyone poses for the camera.

↓Fishguard harbour, opened in 1906, was the creation of the GWR and the Irish Great Southern & Western Railway. It was a major investment aimed at trans-Atlantic trade, and boat trains ran from 1908. The last liner called in 1926, after which the emphasis switched to local trade.

←The line from Carmarthen to Aberystwyth was essentially rural, yet carried heavy holiday and freight traffic. Pencader, seen here on a summer's day in the 1950s, was the junction for the Newcastle Emlyn branch.

↓A small station on a busy line, Cockett was between Swansea and Llanelli. In the early 1960s an engineering train pauses at the platform. The station name is depicted in white-painted bricks, and there is plenty of GWR detail to be seen.

←Bargoed is a Valleys Line station, once busy with coal traffic. Here, it is May 2005 and Class 37 No. 37425 is still carrying snowploughs. The signalman is waiting to receive the single-line token from its driver. By then high-visibility jackets were standard for railway staff.

↑The Chester & Holyhead Railway was one of Britain's first great main lines, and its legacy lives on in the engineering and in many of the buildings. Bangor station, sandwiched between two tunnels, is a grand structure in brick and white stone designed by Francis Thompson and opened in 1848. In 1961 an LMS Black Five, No. 45390, waits outside the station.

↘ In August 1959 Royal Scot Class No. 46139, 'The Welch Regiment', waits at Rhyl with a London-bound express. The large station, completely rebuilt in 1901 and still largely unchanged, reflects the importance of holiday traffic on the North Wales coast.

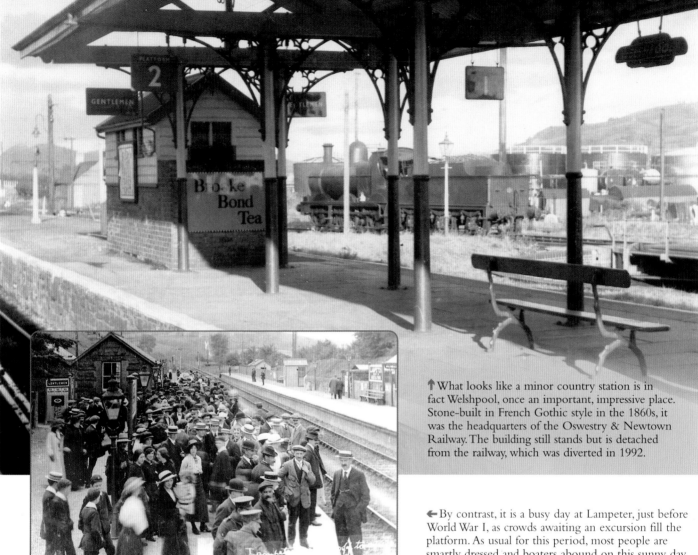

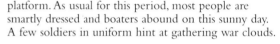

What looks like a minor country station is in fact Welshpool, once an important, impressive place. Stone-built in French Gothic style in the 1860s, it was the headquarters of the Oswestry & Newtown Railway. The building still stands but is detached from the railway, which was diverted in 1992.

By contrast, it is a busy day at Lampeter, just before World War I, as crowds awaiting an excursion fill the platform. As usual for this period, most people are smartly dressed and boaters abound on this sunny day. A few soldiers in uniform hint at gathering war clouds.

From 1961 the Blue Pullman network was extended to Wales, with the introduction of the daily South Wales Pullman linking London and Swansea. All Blue Pullmans were withdrawn in May 1973, and this evening view at Swansea could show the final run of a commemorative train shortly after that date.

↑Newport station has enjoyed a chequered history. Brunel's original, wood-covered train shed was swept away during a complete rebuilding of the station by the GWR in 1878. The platforms and canopies shown here date from that time; a GWR bench underlines the period look.

→Rebuilt again in 1930, when the GWR added the rather gaunt brick block in a vague classical style that still dominates the site, Newport has now been transformed by the addition of a new concourse and bridge at the western end, completely changing the station's layout.

↘Enthusiasts gather at Newport to greet the arrival of a Class 57 diesel locomotive and matching train in a new Arriva Trains Wales livery. Having been threatened with extinction, locomotive-hauled passenger trains are now making a bit of a comeback.

↗ A Cardiff-bound HST 125 unit moves out of Newport, drawing away from the station's new buildings, completed in 2010. A space-age look and space-age technology in the plastic ETFE material used for the cladding make it exciting, though apparently no attempt has been made to relate it to the earlier parts of the station.

↓ Abergavenny station, known as Monmouth Road until the town's other station, Brecon Road, closed in 1958, is little changed from the 1850s, when it was built. Constructed from reddish stone, it echoed the then fashionable Italian villa style. GWR benches and a pleasant independent café add to the appeal. In early 2011, a train from Hereford pauses at the opposite platform, where there is still a proper waiting room.

FAMOUS PLACES
BARMOUTH BRIDGE

Judging by the number of postcards sent over the years, Barmouth bridge, with Cader Idris and the Mawddach estuary, must be one of the most popular views in Wales. This extraordinary structure was opened in 1867, crossing the estuary on 113 spans of 18ft each. It was built entirely of wood, apart from the iron spans at the Barmouth end, one of which could be opened for shipping. These were replaced by steel ones, but otherwise the bridge is as first built, and is the longest wooden railway bridge in Britain. It still has the original footbridge, which offers glorious views.

←↓ These Edwardian artist-drawn cards are typical of hundreds of popular images of Barmouth bridge and the estuary. It is hard to find cards that do not include the bridge, demonstrating how Victorian engineering often added to the landscape.

Barmouth. — The Bridge.

BARMOUTH VIADUCT AND CADER IDRIS. A 293

↘ In misty conditions, a steam-hauled enthusiasts' special makes its way slowly across the bridge in 1987, hauled by a GWR veteran. The train is crossing the 1899 steel spans, the nearest of which was built to open for shipping. Opening it was a laborious procedure, involving eight men with crank handles swinging the span sideways on its central pier. Luckily, demand was limited, and the bridge has not been opened for decades.

➡This Edwardian card used an old photograph of the bridge, showing the original iron spans before they were replaced in 1899. As the pictures here show, this has always been the favourite viewpoint, with Cader Idris forming the backdrop.

BARMOUTH BRIDGE.

8097

⬇This is a slightly later version of the same view, with the steel spans in place. It also shows the sharp curve of the elevated track as it turns towards Barmouth station.

⬇A more unusual and later version, perhaps of the 1930s, shows the view from the other side. With its focus on the bridge, this gives a sense of its length, some 800 yards.

THE VIADUCT FROM PANORAMA WALK, BARMOUTH.

⬅With a typical Barmouth terrace in the background, a local train sets off across the bridge in the 1920s. The footpath was part of the original structure and is still there, offering an exciting walk and spectacular views. As the meeting place of the coastal routes and the line inland to Bala and Corwen, Barmouth was in its heyday a busy station with the bridge in continuous use. Today, it is rather quieter.

TUNNELS, BRIDGES & VIADUCTS

The landscape of Wales represented a great challenge to Victorian railway engineers and builders, but this did not deter them from creating an extensive network of lines that linked most parts of the principality. As a result, the railways of Wales have always been famous for their tunnels, bridges and other impressive engineering features, some of which were seen as wonders of the world when first built. Line closures have reduced the lists, but some of these structures survive in use and others can still be appreciated. Their scenic quality and their landscape setting meant that they were frequently used as subjects for postcards.

↘ Newport station has always been one of the busiest in Wales, resulting in a long history of rebuilding and redevelopment. At the western end are two tunnels, one from 1848 and the other from 1911.

↑ The Chester & Holyhead Railway was one of Britain's first great trunk routes and its engineering reflected the genius of Robert Stephenson. This postcard shows the stone viaduct over the Dingle in Old Colwyn.

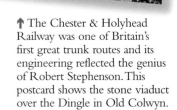

➡Robert Stephenson's 1850 Britannia Bridge over the Menai Straits was one of the greatest engineering achievements of the early railway age. This Victorian view shows the piers carrying rectangular wrought-iron tubes, through which the trains ran. After a fire in 1970, the bridge was rebuilt without the tubes.

← Striding side by side across the valley of the Ceiriog at Chirk are Thomas Telford's aqueduct, built in 1801 to carry the Llangollen Canal, and Henry Robertson's 1848 viaduct for the Shrewsbury & Chester Railway. This famous postcard view celebrates their achievement. Both the aqueduct and the viaduct are still in use.

→ Crumlin viaduct was demolished in 1966, but this postcard from the early 1900s shows the delicate majesty of this remarkable structure in lace-like wrought iron. When opened in 1857, it pioneered the use of the Warren truss and was, at 200ft, one of the highest viaducts in the world.

Crumlin Viaduct.

← The famously elegant Cefn viaduct was completed in 1848. Its 19 limestone arches, carrying the railway 146ft above the Dee, made it the longest in Britain at the time.

→ This Victorian pamphlet reflects the contemporary enthusiasm for the Menai bridges. It gives the details so much appreciated by tourists in that era, such as weight, height, materials and cost. For example, there are 2 million rivets in Britannia Bridge, and the lions at each end are 12ft 8ins high.

DIMENSIONS & PARTICULARS

OF THE

Menai Suspension

AND

Britannia Tubular

Bridges

OVER THE Menai Straits

PRICE ONE PENNY

GOODS TRAINS

Some of the earliest railways in Wales were horse-drawn tramways linking coal mines or slate quarries to canal wharfs and coastal harbours. These set a pattern with mineral traffic, and particularly coal, being the driving force behind much of the Welsh railway network during the 19th century. Until the 1960s, industry remained dominant in Wales, though the remote and scattered nature of much of the country meant that many communities were dependent on the railways for the maintenance of commercial, agricultural, domestic and social life.

← In May 1958, two GWR heavy goods tank locomotives, a Class 5100 and a Class 4200, drag a long, mixed freight away from the Severn tunnel. Until the 1970s the main route in and out of Wales for much of the country's goods traffic was via the tunnel, so sights like this were commonplace.

↙ The Cambrian main line via Talerddig was challenging. In the 1960s, this British Railways Standard Class 4 locomotive, No. 75047, approaches the top of Talerddig Bank with a mixed freight.

→In South Wales coal was king until the 1980s. This photograph, taken in 1982, shows a Class 37 diesel approaching Newport station at the head of a long train of empty coal wagons, probably on its way to the Severn tunnel. Within a few years the South Wales coal industry had been decimated, and scenes like this became quite rare.

↑It is 1990, and new freight liveries have appeared on the network. Here, a pair of Class 37 diesels in Railfreight general duties colours head a train of empty coal hoppers near Pencoed, between Cardiff and Bridgend.

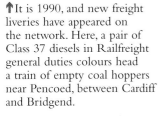

↘Large freight yards and distribution areas were a feature of the South Wales coal lines. This is Aberbeeg in May 1975, with two Class 37 diesels at work sorting and moving empty coal wagons.

↓Managing the general goods traffic was a daily challenge for the railways everywhere. This is at Tenby in the 1960s. The signalman keeps a watchful eye while he holds a mixed freight on the main line. Meanwhile, shunting operations continue.

SHEDS & WORKS

The intricate railway network of South Wales was created largely for the coal trade, which was to dominate the region until the latter part of the 20th century. Dense traffic required large numbers of locomotives, so sheds in this area were thick on the ground, with some mining and industrial centres requiring more than one. In relative terms, just a handful of railway sheds served the rest of Wales. In the British Railways era these were divided, for historical reasons, between the London Midland and the Western regions. Despite the large number of independent companies that contributed to the making of the Welsh network, there were only a few locomotive works in the country. Most began to disappear with the dominance of the GWR and the LNWR during the late 19th century, and little manufacturing survived into the 1920s.

↑A large Class 7200 2-8-2 tank locomotive, No. 7203, rests in Newport shed in the 1950s, with a plentiful supply of lamps. These heavy-duty locomotives are typical of those being built for the coal trade in the early 20th century.

→Wrexham shed served both a rural area in the centre and northeast of Wales and the needs of local industry. By the time this photograph was taken, the buildings had seen better days and British Railways was scaling things down.

→ In British Railways days the old stone-built Danygraig shed was home predominantly to a considerable number of tank locomotives, engaged mostly in the coal and docks traffic around the Swansea area.

← Looking clean and tidy in the sunshine, Aberdare shed was a classic roundhouse. Lined up on the day this photograph was taken are six GWR locomotives, mostly members of heavy tank classes designed for the coal trade.

→ Caerphilly works, one of the most important in Wales, was built in 1899 by the Rhymney Railway and taken over by the GWR in 1923. For much of its life it was involved in the repair, maintenance and refurbishing of locomotives, carriages and wagons, though some mineral wagons were built here. It survived into the British Railways era, and was eventually closed in 1963.

← Not much was happening at Carmarthen shed when this photographer visited in the 1950s. There are no locomotives in steam and the shed looks half empty. Several GWR classes are represented.

ALONG MAIN LINES
CENTRAL ENGLAND

G.C. Railway.—Manchester Express passing Rickmansworth.

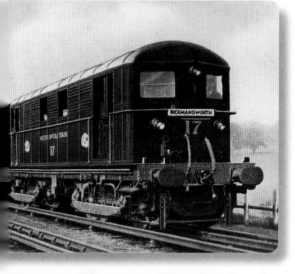

TRAIN SCENES

Central England is a large area, of great diversity in terms of geography and landscape and closely packed with cities, towns and villages. The railway map of this area was also dense and complex, at least until the 1960s, when much was lost. The main lines have always tended to run in a north–south direction, linked by a network of lesser lines and rural routes running across the country. These were built in a rather piecemeal way, to satisfy the changing demands of passengers, industry, commerce and agriculture. The region also includes some of Britain's earliest railways, reflecting the growth of industrial production and manufacture during the Victorian era. As a result, the legacy of railway photographs from Central England is particularly rich.

← As is apparent from most chapters in this book, railway photographers greatly preferred to take pictures of oncoming trains, mainly in order to focus on the locomotive. This photograph, of a GWR Birmingham-bound train near Brill & Ludgershall station in June 1935, features instead the varied coaching stock and the Buckinghamshire landscape.

↓ Another classic GWR scene is this hand-tinted photograph, entitled 'Waiting for the Right Away at Badminton Station'. The date is July 1948, so it is actually a British Railways scene, though filled with GWR details.

← The defining qualities of the GWR are familiar because so much survived unchanged into the BR era. Here, Grange Class locomotive No. 6871, 'Bourton Grange', the station name board, the signal box and the general ambience are all pure GWR, yet the scene is 1964, with a Weymouth-bound express racing through Aynho under a threatening sky.

➜ This 1920s photograph shows a Wolverhampton-to-Paddington express leaving Stourbridge Junction, in the care of a very smart but elderly 4-4-0 Bulldog Class locomotive, No. 3308, 'Falmouth'.

➘ Passenger steam haulage from Birmingham ended in March 1967. This photograph, taken near West Bromwich, shows Castle Class No. 7029, 'Clun Castle', doing everything it can to make the last steam working from Birmingham entirely unforgettable.

←Signals provide a frame for this view of an A4-headed express racing through Hertfordshire on its way towards Kings Cross.

↑Beneath clouds of dense black smoke, and certainly not reflecting the purity associated with its name, ex-LMS Patriot Class locomotive No. 45519, 'Lady Godiva', works through the demanding Pennine landscape near Dore and Totley in the 1950s.

↓A young enthusiast, standing on the parapet of the southern portal of Hadley Wood tunnel in the 1950s, has a perfect view of an Edinburgh-bound express and its rather unkempt A3 Class locomotive.

←This classic scene is from a 1920s postcard, showing the 10.25am St Pancras-to-Manchester express approaching Bakewell, in Derbyshire. The locomotive, described in the caption as 'a reliable type', is a 3-cylinder Midland compound.

↑The water troughs and cutting at Bushey were always a popular location with photographers. A typical product is this 1950s view of an ex-LMS Patriot taking water at speed.

→It is the holiday season in 1962 and Jubilee Class locomotive No. 45690, 'Leander', makes a smoky start from Chester, with a long summer excursion from Manchester to Bangor in North Wales. It would not have been known at that time, but 'Leander' was destined for preservation.

145

⬆ All trains leaving London's northern termini make their way through Central England to their destinations. In 1962 the diesel-hauled Sheffield Pullman climbs Holloway Bank in north London.

⬇ Another Kings Cross departure, the 5.00pm express to Edinburgh, sets off one sunny evening in May 1976, at the start of a long, hot summer. A Class 55 Deltic diesel is in charge, No. 55003, 'Meld'.

 Framed by the clutter of gantries, support poles and power lines, a Class 86 electric locomotive begins the descent of Camden Bank on its return to Euston in 1973.

↓ With the then little-used Sharpness Docks branch in the foreground, a Class 46 diesel, No. 46047, takes the Liverpool-to-Plymouth train past Berkeley Road Junction, in Gloucestershire, in March 1975. There were 56 of these locomotives, built between 1961 and 1963. Withdrawals began in 1977, making it a short-lived class.

← Much longer lived were the Class 50s. Here, in April 1982, No. 50003, 'Temeraire', waits at Leamington Spa with a Liverpool-to-Paddington train. The locomotive is finished in the so-called Large Logo livery of the early 1980s.

AT THE STATION

Spreading from Wales to East Anglia and from north London to the north Midlands, Central England is a huge and heavily populated region. The dense railway network that served the region included both the first and the last of Britain's great main lines, along with other routes built by a rich variety of companies, large and small. Their legacy is an equally rich variety of stations. Some of these have survived into the 21st century, having been successfully adapted to modern network needs, while others have disappeared, along with the routes that they served. The photographs shown on the following pages reflect these changes, as well as the transition from steam power to diesel, which appears to have captured the imagination of a generation of railway enthusiasts and photographers in the heart of England.

← In 1960 a number of the GWR's famous streamlined railcars were still in service, including this example leaving Great Malvern station on its way to Worcester. The first was introduced in 1934. Later models were designed to operate as two- or three-car units. The poster for Ben Hur enlivens the empty platform.

↑ In 1962 classic GWR locomotives were still dominant on many of the Western Region's routes in Central England. A typical location for them was Worcester Shrub Hill, on the Hereford-to-Paddington line, where sightings such as this Hall Class No. 4913, 'Baglan Hall', were a daily occurrence.

← In 1969 the Class 45 diesel was a common sight on routes linking the North and South of England. This is No. 23, later 45017, leaving Gloucester Eastgate with a train from Newcastle to Bristol. The level crossing, one of several in the city, was famous for the traffic disruption it caused. It was one of the reasons for the closure of Eastgate station in December 1975.

↓ Six years earlier another famous diesel type, a Western Region Warship, No. D828, 'Magnificent', hauls another train through England, in this case from Plymouth to Liverpool and Glasgow. This is Whitchurch, Shropshire, and an intrepid enthusiast has gone down the platform slope to capture his shot, ignored by a railwayman.

Three companies, later merging to form the Midland Railway, came to Derby by 1840. After the merger an impressive station with an exceptionally long facade, shown here in an Edwardian postcard, was designed by Francis Thompson. It survived until World War II, when bombing destroyed much of it.

↑ Until the 1960s Hereford was a major rail centre and the meeting point for several lines. Here, in 1958, station staff and the train crew pass the time of day on the otherwise deserted platform while GWR Class 4300 No. 6352 waits to depart.

→ Another Midlands town with an important railway history was Nottingham. It originally had four stations, the last to be built being the Great Central's Victoria, in 1900. This closed in 1967, but was still busy in 1963, when this photograph was taken of a train entering the station, hauled by Class 4MT No. 43063.

LEEK STATION.

← In the Edwardian era, when this card was produced, Leek was the meeting point for four lines. It was a busy place for both passengers and goods, particularly coal from local pits and the products of the town's textile industry. Today, Leek has no trains at all, and little survives to indicate the town's railway past.

↓ Perhaps the best station in the Midlands is Stoke-on-Trent's great Tudor-style palace, designed by HA Hunt for the North Staffordshire Railway and completed in 1848. The exciting brick and stone facade introduces the splendid train shed. By the mid-1960s electrification was on its way but, as this view shows, little had changed.

←By 1960 diesels were becoming more frequent on the main lines, but steam was still dominant at Crewe. In this November view, an old LMS Jubilee, No. 45571, 'South Africa', waits to depart with a train for Blackpool. To the left, another Jubilee rests between duties. The diesel hides in the shadows.

↓The GWR opened Snow Hill in the 1850s and it quickly developed into Birmingham's second station. This 1962 photograph shows the interior after the 1912 rebuilding. A Blue Pullman attracts attention as it calls on its way to London.

→Here, in March 1960, a GWR King Class locomotive, No. 6001, 'King Edward VII', takes a London train out of Snow Hill. The station was then fully used, but traffic declined from the mid-1960s and it was closed in 1972 and demolished, only for British Rail to rebuild a new Snow Hill on the site in the 1980s.

⬆A couple of passengers walk towards the DMU waiting to depart for Leicester in 1959, surrounded by the muddle and clutter that Birmingham's New Street station then represented. Soon all this was to disappear, to be replaced by a completely new station in 1967.

⬇Operating efficiency was the driving force behind the redevelopment of New Street station, yet on this November day in 1978 something seems to have gone wrong as various locomotives fill the platforms. Four classes are present, 45, 46, 50 and 85.

➜Always a smart station, Leamington Spa has recently undergone a facelift, with a feature made of many of the 1930s GWR details. Gardening has also made a return and these two women seem to be enjoying the platform planting and the miniature floral train while they wait for their train on an early summer morning.

←In this timeless platform scene, a train waits while two women discuss their shopping and two students in the foreground catch up with their work. The setting is Hereford, in March 2011.

⬇Hereford station sits behind the grand buildings to the left, a richly decorated Tudor-style structure of brick and cream stone completed in 1855. Gables, finials, Venetian windows and tall chimneys abound, marking a fitting arrival point for a cathedral city. Sadly, little of this attractive building is now in railway use, and the station itself has seen better days.

⬆Decorative ironwork and fine stonework details reveal the Victorian origins of Loughborough station. It was built by the Midland Railway in 1872 and named accordingly, when Loughborough had two mainline stations. On a spring day in 2011, the platform is empty and the train departs. The despatcher, his job done, turns to go back to his office.

➡Modern station life is all about timetables, digital displays and coming to terms with the complex and sometimes conflicting nature of train operating companies. This girl, seeking information, and maybe inspiration, considers the electronic information panels on Northampton station.

FAMOUS PLACES

MONSAL DALE

The Midland Railway was formed in 1844 from an amalgamation of smaller companies, and soon became ambitious. A route southwards to London was planned, authorized in 1863 and finally opened in 1868. It was a famously expensive enterprise, requiring numerous tunnels and viaducts. Particularly challenging was the route through the Peak District, which faced not only geographical difficulties, but also the fervent opposition of the critic John Ruskin, who feared the destruction of Derbyshire's 'divine' landscape.

Twin viaducts spanned the river Wye at Miller's Dale, but much more famous was the one across Monsal Dale, called Headstone viaduct. The five stone arches are now seen as a vital part of the landscape they threatened to destroy. The line closed in 1968, and is now part of the Monsal Trail.

↓This is the view of the Monsal Dale viaduct that has graced thousands of postcards. This example was issued by the Midland Railway itself in the Edwardian era, to promote what it called 'The Best Route for Comfortable Travel and Picturesque Scenery'.

↘Taken shortly before the line's closure in 1968, this unusual photograph of a diesel-hauled passenger train on the Monsal Dale, or Headstone, viaduct shows the valley's wooded setting and the views enjoyed by generations of passengers. The drama of the journey through the Dales was also heightened by tunnels, with Headstone tunnel opening almost directly onto the viaduct.

Monsal Dale in the Peak District National Park

DERBYSHIRE

See Britain by Train

BRITISH RAILWAYS

↑ This 1930s postcard shows a different perspective, concentrating on the Wye valley away from the viaduct, which is just visible to the left.

↑ Before they closed it, British Railways were well aware of the scenic qualities of the Midland route through Derbyshire. This early 1960s poster features an artistic vision of the viaduct and the Wye valley, with a picturesque quality that might have appealed to John Ruskin.

↓ In September 1951 a loaded ballast train was captured, as it crossed the viaduct, from a viewpoint popular with visitors and walkers today.

↑ This photograph, probably dating from the 1950s, shows the viaduct and the railway in the setting of Monsal Dale and illustrates how responsive Victorian engineers could be to the landscape across which they were building their lines.

TUNNELS, BRIDGES & VIADUCTS

The diverse landscape of central England, with ranges of hills and wide river valleys, demanded of the railway builders some of Britain's most impressive tunnels and viaducts. Several tunnels are more than 2 miles long, with Totley, at 3 miles 950 yards, being Britain's second longest. The difficulties experienced in building these is well known, starting with Stephenson's titanic struggles at Kilsby. Viaducts and bridges also often reflect the way engineers overcame challenges, while exploiting their innate sense of style.

SEVERN BRIDGE.

↑ One of Britain's more unusual viaducts carried a single-track railway over the Severn from Sharpness to near Lydney. It was opened in 1879, to cater for the coal trade. This 1903 card shows the span that swung over the Gloucester & Sharpness Canal. In October 1960 two out-of-control petrol barges hit the bridge, destroying two spans. Never reopened, the bridge was demolished in 1969.

↑ In the autumn of 1983 a British Rail Class 86 electric locomotive hauls its train across the handsome stone arches of the Dutton viaduct over the river Weaver. Completed in 1837 for the Grand Junction Railway, it was designed by the engineer Joseph Locke.

↖ In 1961 an evening train from Stratford-upon-Avon crosses the Worcester & Birmingham Canal on its way into Worcester Foregate Street station. The elegance of the brick bridge, emphasized by the generous piercing, is in contrast to the lumpy canal bridges beyond.

↑This 1909 card shows an
LNWR express emerging from Watford tunnel.
The classical portico is depicted in JC Bourne's famous
1837 lithographs of the London & Birmingham Railway.

↑Smoke and steam pour out
of the portal as a GWR Class
2251 0-6-0 locomotive banks
a freight train into Brunel's
Chipping Camden tunnel.

→A series of parallel tunnels,
the first cut in 1837, carry
the London-to-Birmingham
main line through hills at
Northchurch, Berkhamsted.
In 1957 Class 5MT No. 45004
hauls a local from the tunnel.

↓The Midland Railway route
over the Derbyshire Dales
included Miller's Dale tunnel,
seen here in 1956 as a push-
pull local in the charge of a
Class 2 tank emerges.

GOODS TRAINS

The heart of England was, until the 1960s, a dense mass of interconnecting lines built both to feed goods traffic into the main routes and to serve local industry. Mineral traffic was always important, and to some extent remains so today, despite the fact that the transport of coal has greatly diminished.

Stone and aggregate, clay, oil and chemical industries were all wholly dependent on the railways. At the same time, the network served the needs of local industry, commerce and the retail trade, with both local and long-distance mixed-freight trains being a regular sight well into the 1970s. Nowadays, as elsewhere, container traffic rules.

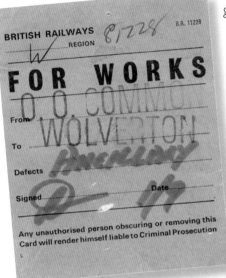

BRITISH RAILWAYS .... REGION   81228   B.R. 11228

FOR WORKS

From

To

Defects

Signed .... Date ....

Any unauthorised person obscuring or removing this Card will render himself liable to Criminal Prosecution

→ In April 1957 an ancient GWR Class 2800 2-8-0 heavy goods locomotive hauls a long, mixed-freight train over the Rowington water troughs, north of Hatton. This classic goods train scene, once commonplace all over the network, is now seen only in re-creations on preserved lines.

↖ GWR No. 3030, a member of the class of locomotives originally built for military use by the Railway Operating Division from 1917, makes light work of a coal train near Leamington Spa in 1928.

BRITISH TRANSPORT COMMISSION
BRITISH RAILWAYS
USE BLOCK LETTERS
B.R. 21202/924
19

From DEEPFIELDS & COSELEY
STEWARTS & LLOYDS LTD. SPRING VALE SIDINGS

25231
HOT SLAG
Blast Furnace

To WELLINGBOROUGH
WELLINGBOROUGH IRON CO'S SIDING
MID Section
Via MARKET HARBOROUGH
NORTHAMPTON

Letter Wagon | Number | 2 | Crane Traffic
Container | | | Gross Weight / Heaviest

Contents SLAG
Consignee WELLINGBOROUGH IRON CO.

→By 1975 there was little regular traffic on the river Weaver, and the barges moored by Frodsham quay seem to have been idle for some time. In the background an oil train bound for Ellesmere Port crosses the central spans of Frodsham viaduct in the care of a Class 25 diesel. The 23 arches of the 1850 viaduct dominate the river valley.

↑On a bright September day in 1964 Modified Hall Class No. 7918, 'Rhose Wood Hall', fills the Gloucestershire skies with smoke as it hauls a long train of empty mineral wagons along the winding valley between Gloucester and Kemble, beside the derelict canal.

↗In 1972 another Class 25 diesel hauls a short pick-up freight from Stoke towards Crewe along the link line from Kidsgrove. These locomotives, a design dating from 1961, were popularly known as 'rats' because they could be seen all over Britain.

LOCOMOTIVE SHEDS

When the British Railways steam era was at its peak, there were over 60 locomotive sheds in central England. Several of the larger towns and cities had more than one shed. With the final demise of mainline steam in 1968, the majority of those that survived were quickly closed and subsequently demolished. A very few were adapted for diesel use and were renamed Motive Power Depots. Photographs of steam sheds in Central England therefore record, in detail, a way of life that was taken for granted at the time but is now virtually extinct.

↗ In the 1970s Shrewsbury shed remained in use to house a variety of diesel locomotives, mostly the ubiquitous Class 47. By this time, the buildings were almost derelict, with gaping holes in the roofs.

↓ Before the Great Central, Woodford Halse was a small town in rural Northamptonshire. The GCR turned it into an important railway town and junction, with the substantial engine shed shown here in an Edwardian postcard view. When the line closed, Woodford reverted to its previous, quieter life.

↓ This is an evocative and soon-to-be-forgotten scene, in Saltley shed in 1963. A Stanier 5MT and a much more recent BR 9F stand at the turntable, the latter being prepared for work by the driver.

↙ Always an important railway centre, Leicester was until the early 1920s served by two companies, the Midland and the Great Central. This shows a typically busy day in the former Midland shed in the British Railways era.

↓ Mechanical coal hoists were increasingly used at major sheds from the 1930s. This cigarette card shows an LMS example at Cricklewood, with a Garratt being coaled. This hoist could hold 500 tons of coal and could load a tender in three minutes.

MECHANICAL COALING

↑ A famous name in steam days, Toton, near Nottingham, has remained a busy depot. The tradition of open days has been maintained; this is the programme for August 1998.

→ This late 19th-century photograph shows the Midland Railway roundhouse at Derby, a classic example of this traditional style of shed with the locomotive bays ranged round a central turntable.

RAILWAY WORKS

Some of the earliest, and some of the best known, railway works are in central England, notably Wolverton, which opened in 1838, and Crewe, Derby and Wolverhampton, all of which were in operation before 1850. Also associated with the region were some of the major names in rolling stock construction, for example the Metropolitan Railway Carriage and Wagon Company, originally established in Saltley, near Birmingham, in 1845. Mergers and rationalization steadily reduced the number of works, particularly after the formation of the Big Four in 1923, and this process continued during the British Railways era. By the time British Rail Engineering had been formed, only Derby and Crewe works survived.

⬇ After many delays, a national steam locomotive testing station was finally opened at Rugby in 1948. This shows a newly built British Railways Standard Class 5 locomotive being tested on the rollers.

➡ This 1930s cigarette card shows wind tunnel testing at the LMS's Research Laboratory at the Derby works. This was a means of improving the design and performance of streamlined locomotives.

WIND TUNNEL

↑Opened in 1840, Derby soon became the major works for the Midland Railway. It retained its importance in the LMS and British Railways eras, with the last steam locomotive being built there in 1957. Today, it is one of the few places in Britain still associated with the building of railway vehicles.

ERECTING SHOP, CREWE WORKS.

↑Crewe's history dates back to 1843, when a small Cheshire village became the site of one of Britain's biggest and most famous railway works, developed initially by the LNWR. This postcard from about 1905 shows the main locomotive erecting shop.

↑The last locomotive to be built by the GWR at Wolverhampton left the works in 1908. This 1950s photograph, taken on an open day, shows that maintenance and overhaul were the primary functions of most works.

←HST 125 trains went into service in the early 1970s, revolutionizing high-speed rail travel in Britain. This June 1972 British Rail press photograph shows the prototype power car in Derby works, ready for the first track trials. The front was subsequently redesigned.

G.E.R. Express

ALONG MAIN LINES
EASTERN ENGLAND

"Continental Express" G.E.R.

G. E. Ry. Norfolk Coast Express.

FAIR BE ALL YOUR PATHS
AND PROSPEROUS YOUR LIFE

Southend - Fenchurch Street Express
4·4·2/T No 80 "Thundersley"

TRAIN SCENES

Until the closures of the 1960s, eastern England abounded in rural railways and branch lines, with only a few main lines forming the backbone of the network. With the exception of the old Midland & Great Northern route across Norfolk, these are still in place, though in some cases less busy, chiefly because of the great reduction in freight traffic. Holiday traffic, once the mainstay of some lines, has also greatly diminished. At the same time, modernization and electrification have brought new business to the core lines, London to Norwich and London to Cambridge and Kings Lynn. Also improved are suburban services and routes eastwards from Peterborough, all of which are featured here.

↑In the 1950s a Cambridge-bound train climbs past Potters Bar, headed by a B17, or Sandringham, Class locomotive, No. 61623, 'Lambton Castle'. The design dates from 1928, but most were built later. This one, for example, had a short life, from 1943 to 1959.

↑Many modern trains operate as fixed units, making station shunting operations redundant. The pilot locomotive, once a permanent fixture at large stations, is now extinct. This 1910 photograph shows a Victorian veteran engaged in pilot duties at Norwich Thorpe.

↘ One of Britain's most famous preserved locomotives is Great Northern Railway No. 1, Patrick Stirling's great express locomotive of 1870. An early candidate for preservation, this has always been popular, as indicated by the crowds at Peterborough in 1938, when No. 1 was heading a special for the Railway Correspondence and Travel Society.

↗ The Eastern Counties
Railway built the first
station at March in 1847,
but this photograph shows
the much larger one opened
in 1882, after the GNR and
the GER turned March into
a major junction. On a quiet
day in 1962, an LNER Class A2,
No. 60500, 'Edward Thompson', takes
its train through the empty platforms.

← This serves as a reminder
of the frequency of restaurant
cars on many routes until
the 1970s. The journey from
London to Cambridge was
never much more than an
hour, yet there was time to
enjoy a meal. Today, there is
only the at-seat trolley service.

↓ The LNER's B12 Class
locomotives were developed
from an old Great Eastern
design. This 1950 photograph
shows No. 61557 heading
an express at Mark's Tey, the
junction for the Sudbury line.
By 1959 only eight of the
81 built were still in service.

← Once Yarmouth had three stations, Vauxhall, South Town and Beach. In 1979 there was only one, but Vauxhall was still on the lighting columns. An arrival from London, a Class 37 diesel, then the mainstay of East Anglian traffic, propels the empty stock to the carriage sidings.

↓ Also in 1979, another Class 37 brings a train from Yarmouth past Trowse junction on its way into Norwich. The London line swings away to the right. A busy yard, lots of semaphore signals and an active signal box underline the traditional railway look.

↓ In 1959 the railway scene was much more varied. Former LNER carriages were still in use, and diesels were quite rare. This London-bound train is leaving Ely headed by a Brush Type 2, or Class 30, diesel, No. D5508. The first of these locomotives were built in 1957. All were based in East Anglia and had been withdrawn by 1970. Further development led to the very successful Class 31.

← In East Anglian terms, the line from Bury St Edmunds to Long Melford was busy but, except in World War II, hardly a main line. In April 1961, the month of closure to passengers, a DMU pauses at Lavenham. Staff outnumber passengers.

↓ Several named trains operated on the main lines of eastern England, including the Fenman to Kings Lynn. However, this one, hauled by a Class 47 and with its Bulmer's Pullman, is probably a special rail tour.

↑ Driver comfort was one of the issues motivating the switch from steam to diesel and electric power. This Metro Cammell works photograph shows the cab on DMU units built for the Cambridge service.

↓ By 1989 a range of new trains for suburban and main lines were in service. Here, a Class 315 EMU in Network SouthEast livery enters Liverpool Street on a sunny Saturday morning. These trains were built in York from 1980 to 1981.

AT THE STATION

Apart from the main lines from London to Cambridge, Kings Lynn, the Essex coast resorts, Norwich and the Norfolk coastal ports, the East Anglian railway network was largely suburban or rural. At its peak it was a surprisingly dense network, but it was greatly reduced from the 1960s, particularly in the rural regions, where large areas were left with no rail service. So, although in their heyday the country stations were always busy, serving large but widely scattered communities, there were very few big mainline stations. The Great Eastern was the largest railway company in the region, but there were other mainline operations, including the idiosyncratic Midland & Great Northern Junction Railway's route across Norfolk.

➜ When this photograph was taken in about 1910, Upminster was a rural station, but it was already part of London's expanding commuter network, with both mainline and underground railway connections. With track work going on, and only a few passengers awaiting the train, peak time was clearly well past.

⬇ One of the mainstays of Eastern Region mainline services was the Thompson B1 Class, introduced by the LNER from 1942. Here, on a sunny day in 1959, the driver of No. 61279 is ready to depart from Colchester with a London-bound train, and is looking for the guard's flag. Smoke and steam reflect the fireman's efforts.

Railway Station & Queen's Hotel, Westcliff-on-Sea.

⬆At Wickford Junction, the branch to Burnham-on-Crouch and Southminster leaves the Great Eastern's main line to Southend Victoria. It was never a large station, with its timetables dominated by Essex commuter traffic, yet there were plenty of staff, as this Edwardian photograph indicates.

⬇In the 1980s, Intercity was British Rail's most successful division, and its distinctive livery was seen all over mainline Britain. This is Ipswich, with a London service from Norwich pulling into the platform headed by a Class 86 electric locomotive, No. 86217, then carrying the 'Comet' nameplate.

⬆This Edwardian postcard shows Westcliff-on-Sea station, on the London, Tilbury & Southend Railway's route to Southend Central, at a quiet moment. A London-bound train approaches. Although this was principally a commuter route, the size of the adjoining hotel indicates the popularity of Westcliff and the surrounding area with holidaymakers.

↗Another Thompson B1 locomotive, No. 61046, is seen hard at work in the 1950s shunting goods wagons at Clare station, in Suffolk, on the cross-country route from Cambridge to Colchester. The sidings are full of wagons, indicating the importance of these rural lines to their local community.

↓Today Melton Constable is a small town in the heart of rural north Norfolk, with little to suggest that it was, until 1959, a major junction station and the site of the railway works built by the Midland & Great Northern Junction company. Here, shortly before final closure in 1964, a diesel multiple has arrived.

➡On a busier day at Melton Constable, a British Railways Standard locomotive waits at the head of a mixed freight while the diesel railcar sits in the adjacent platform, ready to depart. The handful of passengers seem hardly to justify the number of carriages lined up in the siding.

← A rare visitor to Norwich, a Deltic diesel locomotive runs round the special train it has just hauled into the station, while enthusiasts lean out to take their photographs. It is a misty day in the 1970s and, considering the interest the visitor might have generated, the adjacent platforms are surprisingly empty.

↓ Cromer Beach, the Norfolk town's second and much more central station, was opened in 1887, significantly helping Cromer to develop as a resort. Small at first, it was later enlarged, as seen here. Always a terminus, it is still in use today, and Sheringham trains have to reverse out.

↘ The railway connecting Bishop's Stortford and Braintree in Essex could hardly be called a main line, yet it carried plenty of traffic. In this 1930s photograph a five-coach passenger train pauses at Takeley station, while a long coal train bound for Braintree disappears into the distance, past some busy factory sidings. It's a scene that underlines the vital role played by the railways in that era.

➔ The modern station is often a colourful and lively place, thanks in part to the varied retail outlets on the platform. This is Ipswich in the summer of 2010 and the train manager is trying to get her London train away on time.

⬇ Ely station opened in 1845 and grew to be a major junction, with lines radiating in six directions. Francis Thompson was the architect, and his simple classicism is still apparent in the main building, seen here across the platforms where waiting passengers enjoy the sunshine.

⬆ Norwich, or Norwich Thorpe as it was called until 1969, is a splendid 1880s terminus station in a French Renaissance style, with a generous concourse and plenty of decorative cast-iron work. On a summer Saturday in 2010, visitors to the city make their way towards the barrier.

⬇➡ The platforms at Norwich are sheltered by the original 1886 decorative awnings in wood and glass. The recently repainted ornamental cast-iron supports were made by the famous local ironworks, Barnard, Bishop & Barnard.

FAMOUS PLACES

HARWICH & PARKESTON QUAY

The Great Eastern Railway first developed Continental steamer traffic from the long-established Essex port of Harwich, opening a hotel in 1865. Limited quayside facilities soon caused problems, and from 1882 the railway created a new international port a mile inland along the Stour estuary. This became known as Parkeston Quay, named after CH Parkes, the GER's chairman. A new hotel was built, and the port expanded rapidly, with both passenger services and train ferries for freight serving north European ports. Now known as Harwich International, it is still a major port.

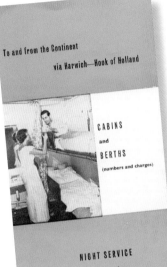

To and from the Continent
via Harwich—Hook of Holland

CABINS
and
BERTHS
(numbers and charges)

NIGHT SERVICE

by s.s. Amsterdam
s.s. Arnhem
s.s. Duke of York

BRITISH RAILWAYS

←The most popular routes to Holland still operate, albeit without the famous boat train connections of the past. This 1960 leaflet promotes the overnight service; a First Class de luxe cabin cost £4.

↘ The Day Continental was one of the famous boat trains from Liverpool Street. Here, in July 1955, a Class B1 locomotive, No. 61233, brings this popular service into Parkeston Quay.

↑A diesel-hauled boat train waits to depart, probably in the late 1960s. The substantial station, notable for its long platforms and classical-style buildings, was called Harwich Parkeston Quay from GER days until it was renamed Harwich International in 1995.

↑←Soon after its formation, the LNER introduced new expresses and boat trains serving Parkeston Quay, one of which, with eleven carriages and two Pullmans, is shown in this image from a promotional card. The routes were extensively advertised with many booklets, including this 1925 illustrated example, reflecting the LNER's famously stylish approach to publicity.

↑As a custom-built international port, Parkeston Quay was well equipped with docks, cranes, sidings and warehouses to cater for the important freight traffic. As well as the fleet of passenger steamers, there were also dedicated freight vessels, including the train ferries, which operated into the 1990s.

→The Parkeston Quay Hotel was opened in 1884 to replace the Great Eastern Hotel on the Harwich Town quay. The large, two-storey structure, with its French-inspired clock tower, flanked the long platform. The hotel was closed in the 1960s and converted into offices.

G.E. RLY. HOTEL & STATION APPROACH, PARKESTON QUAY.

TUNNELS, BRIDGES & VIADUCTS

Much of the landscape of eastern England presented few challenges to Victorian railway engineers and builders so, compared to other parts of Britain, the region has few significant tunnels or viaducts. Indeed, Ipswich is famous for having one of only two tunnels in East Anglia. When the network was at its peak, level crossings were as common as bridges, and former keepers' cottages remain a familiar feature in the landscape. For the same reason, many of the region's rivers and waterways were crossed at low level, resulting in a distinctive series of swing-bridges. Some of these are still in use, underlining the achievements of Victorian engineers.

←This dramatic Edwardian postcard shows a Great Eastern Railway express, hauled by a locomotive sporting the company's famous blue livery, as it emerges from the short tunnel, 361yds long, on the London side of Ipswich station.

↓In 1989 a Norwich-bound express in Intercity livery enters Ipswich station, with the tunnel in the background. The first station at Ipswich was opened in 1847 but was quickly enlarged with a range of Italianate-style buildings. The distinctive ridge-and-furrow platform awnings were added by the GER in 1883.

➜ The Breydon swing-bridge, seen here in the open position, was completed in 1903, with five spans crossing the river Yare near Yarmouth. Signal boxes at each end controlled the single track. Closed to trains in 1953, the bridge was demolished in 1962.

Swing Bridge - Sutton Bridge (Open)

⬆⬊ Sutton bridge, in Lincolnshire, has had three successive bridges over the river Nene. This is the third one, built by the Midland & Great Northern in 1897 as a combined road and rail bridge, with an opening span 176ft long and a raised, central control cabin. It is shown above in open position and (right) closed. After the railway closed in 1959, the bridge was adapted for two-way road use.

The Bridge, Sutton Bridge.

NORWICH ROAD RAILWAY BRIDGE. IPSWICH.

⬆ The popularity of this Edwardian card showing the Norwich Road railway bridge in Ipswich underlines the rarity of such structures in East Anglia. The notice on the bridge encourages tramcar passengers to stay seated while passing under it.

⬆ From the 1840s, the approach to Norwich Thorpe station was via a swing-bridge over the river Wensum at Trowse. This early 20th-century card shows the new double-track bridge, which was completed in 1905.

GOODS TRAINS

In East Anglia the bulk of the goods traffic was agricultural, with seasonal cargoes such as beet, potatoes, grain, peas and flowers being important, along with dairy products. As with other rural regions, local and domestic traffic was always an essential component. Across eastern England as a whole, freight was dominated by traffic to and from the ports, including the daily fish trains. The huge freight concentration yards at Whitemoor, near March, which began to be developed during the 1880s, added significantly to the amount of freight traffic in the region.

↑This 1880 GER waybill offers an insight into the complex nature of freight traffic. By that date, Harwich was a major international port, yet a basket of yeast required the same careful documentation as a trainload of coal or fish.

↓As a meeting point for the eastern and central regions of England, Peterborough was always busy. This is a typical scene from the 1950s, with a Gresley-designed Class V2 locomotive, No. 60902, bringing a goods train through Peterborough North. Two containers head the long line of box vans.

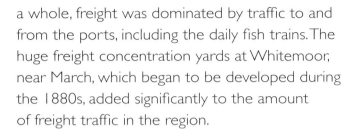

↓Engineering trains were from the early days an important part of the regular pattern of freight traffic in all regions. Here, in March 1977, a Class 47 diesel, No. 47102, hauls a train of loaded ballast hoppers through Southend Central station, in preparation for a weekend track-maintenance programme.

← The sight of a diesel-hauled goods train was still fairly unusual in 1962. Enthusiasts would have been pleased to note this Brush Type 2, Class 31 locomotive, No. D5695, heading a line of plank wagons near Chelmsford.

↑ In 1956 two typical 0-6-0 goods workhorses meet at Whitemoor junction, near March, Cambridgeshire – an LNER J20, No. 64769, from the 1940s, and an old Midland 4F, No. 43870, from 1918.

↘ The Harwich-to-Zeebrugge train ferry started in 1924 and rapidly became Britain's most important route for international freight. This 1930s image shows a line of wagons being unloaded. Services continued until the opening of the Channel Tunnel.

C. M. HAIGH,
Produce Merchant,
Chatteris Station,
Cambs.
..........Bags.   L & N.E. (G.E. Sect.)

SHEDS & WORKS

With few main lines, the railway network of eastern England was over a long period dominated by suburban, commuter and rural routes, along with a complex variety of freight services. The successful operation of this network required a great number of locomotive sheds, only a few of which were of significant size, usually in major centres such as Cambridge, Kings Lynn and Norwich. With the end of steam, most of the smaller sheds quickly disappeared. The Great Eastern Railway's main works was at Stratford, in east London; this survived until 1991.

→ Opened in 1848 by the Eastern Counties Railway, Stratford works later became the Great Eastern Railway's manufacturing base. In 1891 it built a locomotive in 9 hours, 47 minutes, a record that still stands. Later operated by the LNER and BR, it survived as a repair works until 1991.

↘ As the terminus of a busy commuter line, Shoeburyness in Essex had quite a large shed, as this 1950s photograph suggests. At this point the extensive military railway serving the ranges along the east coast was still in use.

→ This busy scene shows Melton Constable shed in rural north Norfolk in the 1930s, when this long-lost rail centre was still at the heart of a complex network. A variety of locomotives crowd the tracks leading into and around the shed. The elaborate lamp is an M&GN relic. Not a trace of this scene remains today.

← By the mid-1960s, diesels had taken over at Kings Lynn and the old steam shed in the background was starting to look decrepit. A Type 2 Brush diesel stands by the redundant water tower, while to the left is a group of shunters used for working the dock lines.

→ By the 1970s, electrification of the main line to Norwich had rendered the former steam shed at Colchester largely superfluous. However, the demands of freight still required the stabling of a variety of diesel locomotives, including Class 08 shunters, as seen in this 1979 view.

↑ By the time these Class 37 diesels were being stabled at Norwich in the summer of 1988, the working days of the city's old steam shed were nothing more than a distant memory.

↑ Dating back to the 1840s, Stratford was one of London's larger sheds. With the end of steam, a new diesel maintenance depot was opened in the early 1960s. This card shows some of its first 'clients'.

ALONG MAIN LINES
NORTHERN ENGLAND

M. Ry. Liverpool and Manchester Express.

HE SIGNAL OF HAPPINESS
E'ER BE SET FOR THEE.

BOARD TO INDICATE CHANGE IN GRADIENT

TELEPHONE BOX WITH DISTINCTIVE MARKING FOR DRIVERS TO SPEAK TO SIGNALMAN WHEN STOPPED AT A SIGNAL OR IN EMERGENCY.

LEVEL 160

ALAN ANDERSON

L.M.S. "CORONATION SCOT" THE NEW RECORD-BREAKING LOCOMOTIVE.
TRAVELS BETWEEN GLASGOW AND LONDON IN 6¼ HOURS.

TRAIN SCENES

The North of England has a spectacular diversity of landscape, and an interesting variety of main lines, but it is the underlying sense of railway history that made it particularly exciting for enthusiasts and photographers alike. The railways were born in the Northeast, and the last steam trains operated by British Rail on the national network ran in the North. It was also a region associated with the first generation of mainline diesel locomotives, equally impressive in such dramatic landscape settings. Northern England was the territory of those great rivals, the LMS and the LNER, whose spirit of competition continued into the British Railways years.

↘ In a classic scene from the last months of the age of steam, an LMS Jubilee Class locomotive, No. 45593, 'Kolhapur', fills its tender from the Garsdale water troughs. This is the 10.17 from Leeds to Glasgow on a misty July morning in 1967, and the enthusiasts are leaning out of the windows to savour to the full a vanishing experience.

→ In the 1930s, rivalry between the LMS and the LNER was intense. This postcard of the time shows the LNER's non-stop London-to-Newcastle express on its 268-mile run. The locomotive is 'Baynardo', a sister to 'Flying Scotsman'.

THE L N E R. NON-STOP KINGS CROSS TO NEWCASTLE PASSING DURHAM CATHEDRAL

↗ On a July Sunday in 1961, engineering work on the main line drives the London express onto a diversionary route via Bishop Auckland. Class A1 No. 60158, 'Aberdonian', hauls the long train up the incline away from the normal route at Relly Mill junction, offering a different view from the window.

↓ Running tender first, an old Class J39 locomotive, No. 64903, banks a rake of carriages up the steep Laisterdyke cutting and through a typical urban landscape away from Bradford Exchange station, while the driver leans well out to keep an eye on things.

↗ In July 1963 a holiday special bound for Blackpool heads south through Tebay station, with the shed and coaling tower in the background. The locomotive is a Patriot, No. 45512, 'Bunsen', from the group rebuilt in the late 1940s from Henry Fowler's original 1930 LMS design.

↓ With smoke and steam concealing its train, a smart-looking Princess Coronation Class locomotive, No. 46229, 'Duchess of Hamilton', hauls the South Yorkshireman through a misty landscape. Introduced in 1948, the South Yorkshireman ran between London and Bradford, following the old Great Central route. After its withdrawal in 1960, the name reappeared in 2008 on an express service connecting St Pancras and Sheffield.

↗ With the Rochdale Canal in the foreground, an enthusiast's special double-headed by a BR Standard and an old LMS 5MT in the centre of the photograph, and the stone terraces and mills of Littleborough in the distance, this 1968 photograph captures wonderfully the industrial history of this part of Lancashire.

↑Class A1 No. 60124, 'Kenilworth', simmers by the turntable outside Darlington shed. The tender is full of coal and water, and the locomotive and its crew, on stand-by duty, are prepared for whatever turns up.

←As the train from Blackpool to Leeds approaches the Copy Pit stretch, the driver leans out of Jubilee No. 45565, 'Victoria', to get a good view of the tunnel. The enthusiasts, enjoying the sun in August 1968, are also getting ready for the tunnel experience.

⬎ In a fine urban railway landscape, the Edinburgh-to-London train takes the grand elevated approach to Newcastle in September 1972, headed by a Class 55 Deltic, 'The Green Howards'.

⬆ In a glorious Westmorland landscape in the summer of 1967, a rather tired-looking British Railways Class 9F locomotive, No. 92016, runs light towards Lancaster and takes the opportunity to pick up water from the Dillicar troughs.

⬎ On 11 August 1968 crowds fill the platform, and part of the track, at Rainhill station to watch the passing of the last steam special run by British Rail – and, with it, the passing of the age of steam.

⬆In August 1977 a northbound Leeds-to-Glasgow train headed by a Class 45 diesel locomotive, No. 45025, races through a typical Pennine landscape towards Stainforth tunnel, near Settle. Introduced from 1962, the Sulzer Class 4, or Peak, diesels were nearing the end by then, and this example was scrapped in 1981.

⬆Near Warrington, a couple of track men, casually dressed by modern Health and Safety standards, stand to watch a smart-looking Class 87 electric locomotive, No. 87014, 'Knight of the Thistle'.

➡Introduced to mark the new Elizabethan era, the Elizabethan was a daily non-stop service linking London and Edinburgh. It was then the world's longest scheduled non-stop service. By the summer of 1962 the new Deltics were in charge. This is D9004, 'Queen's Own Highlander', near Durham.

AT THE STATION

The stations of the North of England are famous for scale and grandeur, architectural adventurousness and a strong sense of history. They reflect the burgeoning wealth of the region during the Victorian period and express the civic pride engendered by the achievements of the railway. Industrial towns and cities needed grand stations to underline their new status. At the same time, the rapid development of leisure activities in the latter part of the century brought another kind of wealth. More recently, many stations have been restored or rebuilt, in most cases without losing their original spirit of enterprise.

⬆ The Midland Railway made its presence felt in Bradford in no uncertain way with a grand station and hotel on Forster Square, though the actual station was under a huge iron train shed behind the facade. Of this 1924 view, only the hotel remains, and the station is now just three platforms, buried away to the right.

↗ With its classical frontage and spectacular, curving iron train shed, Newcastle is both the railway masterpiece of the architect John Dobson and one of Britain's best station experiences. In this evening view in 1975 the train from Edinburgh is about to leave for London, headed by a Class 55 Deltic, No. 55021, 'Argyll and Sutherland Highlander'.

↗ Many views of Newcastle station show the spectacular crossing of tracks and the amazing signal gantry that used to stand at the platform end. This photograph was taken on a quiet, wet day in the 1930s.

↗ The railway reached York in 1839. The original station, by GT Andrews, was a terminus, and the present through station dates from 1876. Its best feature is, like Newcastle's, the magnificent curving iron train shed, shown well in this late 1950s image of the Flying Scotsman passing northwards through the station, with A4 No. 60033, 'Seagull', at its head.

↑ In August 1976 another train bound for Scotland pulls away from York, this time with a later classic locomotive in charge, Class 55 Deltic No. 55009, 'Alycidon'.

← The complex layout of York station is apparent in the background to this early 1960s view of Class A3 No. 60088, 'Book Law', pulling a London-bound express across the points and away from the curving train shed roof.

➡ Under a pattern of light and shade created by the sun shining through the iron and glass roof, Patriot No. 45547, unnamed, waits at Carlisle Citadel station while the stationmaster has a discussion with the driver, probably about timing. Another great northern station, Carlisle was completed in 1850 and subsequently enlarged at least twice to cater for the trains of the seven companies that used it at its peak before World War I.

⬅ This is another, later view of Carlisle, showing the interior of the train shed on a quiet day in 1967. A mother holds her child up for a better view of Jubilee No. 45562, 'Alberta', perhaps explaining that steam locomotives will soon disappear from the BR network.

⬐ With trainspotters watching keenly, a Royal Scot Class locomotive, No. 46138, 'The London Irish Rifleman', rushes its London-bound express through Wigan North Western station in 1958.

←At Doncaster station in the 1970s two young enthusiasts, complete with flares and Qantas flight bag, take a rubbing from an identity plate on the side of Class 55 Deltic No. 55013, 'The Black Watch'. A friend watches from the platform, in a scene made inconceivable today by security cameras and Health and Safety regulations.

↑The guard and a few passengers walk away from the train that has just arrived at Sheffield Victoria station one evening in June 1965. Steam hides the locomotive's identity, beneath a fine array of BR enamel signs. Opened in 1851, Sheffield Victoria closed in 1970, and nothing in this photograph remains.

↑On an October Sunday in 1981, a diverted Glasgow-to-London express is about to enter Bolton station, with a Class 47 diesel hauling the train and its Class 87 electric locomotive over the non-electrified section.

↘Running tender first and with the driver keeping a lookout, Royal Scot Class locomotive No. 46158, 'The Loyal Regiment', banks some empty carriages out of Liverpool Lime Street and into the tunnel towards Edge Hill. A group of trainspotters, standing well down the platform slope, watch the proceedings.

↓The Royal Scot locomotive, No. 46107, 'Argyll and Sutherland Highlander', hauling the 9am train from Liverpool, has failed at Patricroft station and is being pulled away from the carriages by an ex-LNWR Class G2 goods engine. This and the picture on the right, both taken in 1959, tell a not unfamiliar story from the age of steam.

↑After an inevitable wait, a spare engine has been sent from Patricroft shed. Jubilee No. 45733, 'Novelty', backs down towards the carriages in the platform, ready to resume the journey, no doubt to the passengers' relief.

⬇Sheffield's great train shed was removed in the 1950s, but the platforms have not changed greatly and there is still impressive stonework and the old ridge-and-furrow awnings to enjoy. Here, on a quiet day in 2010, just two passengers share the platforms with a modern diesel–electric Class 222 multiple unit.

⬀ Sheffield Midland is now the city's main station. Opened in 1870 and extended in 1904, it was the Midland Railway's largest station after London St Pancras. Recent restoration has highlighted features such as the decorative ironwork, while in the plaza outside a spectacular water wall has been installed.

⬇Leeds is another station that has recently been restored, and the result is a light and airy space with plenty of high-tech features. Thanks to the variety of train operating companies serving Leeds, it is also a very colourful place.

FAMOUS PLACES
SHAP SUMMIT

In July 1844 the first sod of the Lancaster & Carlisle Railway was cut at Shap Summit, which, at 914ft, was the highest point of the planned route. The line was fully opened in December 1846, a great achievement considering the extremely demanding nature of the landscape.

The approach to the summit from the south, with 30 miles of the line being on an incline of up to 1 in 75, was always a great challenge to steam locomotives and their crews, and double-heading and banking were common. The appeal to photographers was obvious. The line was electrified in 1974, and since then the climb to Shap Summit has been memorable only for the spectacular scenery.

↑An early 1900s postcard of an LNWR Experiment Class locomotive tackling Shap, with aerial escort, shows the long popularity of the scene.

→Working hard as it approaches Scout Green signal box, an ex-LMS Stanier tank locomotive banks a freight up Shap in the early 1960s.

↘In 1963 a rather grimy Patriot Class locomotive makes light work of the descent from the summit, through the classic Cumbrian landscape. The climb up to Shap from the north was not so severe, but nevertheless tested the skills of fireman and driver.

↗ By 1967 the writing was on the wall for Tebay, and for the age of steam. The line to Darlington via Stainmore Summit, with its junction at Tebay, closed in January 1962, and the end of steam haulage would render redundant the massive sheds and support facilities. Stations at Tebay and Shap would close, but the important track maintenance yards – visible here as a mineral train headed by a Class 5MT, No. 44911, starts the climb to the summit – would remain.

← Various classes of diesel were put to work on the Shap run. In 1971 this Class 50 was photographed near Grenholme, on the approach to the summit. The driver, who must originally have been a steam man, has time to relax and look out of the window, a great change from the steam age, when his skills would regularly have been tested to the limit.

↑ Diesels were at work on Shap by the early 1960s, and a photographer could capture an interesting mix of motive power in the area. This shows a Class 40 diesel, photographed on the same July day in 1963 as the Patriot on the opposite page, heading south from the summit with an Edinburgh-to-Birmingham train.

TUNNELS, BRIDGES & VIADUCTS

The rugged terrain of the North of England posed great challenges to the railway builders, and their legacy is a wealth of bridges, viaducts and tunnels that includes some of the highest, longest and deepest in Britain. In many cases, engineering knowledge, particularly in the use of cast and wrought iron, was pushed beyond its known limits. Building techniques relied almost entirely on manual skills, yet great care was taken with design, details of finish and decoration, and architectural excellence, despite pressures of time and money. Almost without exception, the great engineering achievements of the railway builders in the North of England make an important contribution to the natural and urban landscapes in which they stand.

⬇ Swing-bridges on railway lines are relatively rare in Britain. One of the better known examples crosses the river Ouse at Selby, on the line between Leeds and Hull. Designed by Thomas Harrison and built in 1891, it pivots on an off-centre support column, seen here in the 1930s during maintenance work. Unusual is the bridge's pagoda-shaped control tower.

➡ A diesel-hauled train exits the Gothic portal of Gisburn tunnel in the 1980s. Opened in 1879, this was built to please Lord Ribblesdale, the local landowner, who insisted that the railway should be hidden from sight where it crossed his land. He also insisted on castellated portals.

FLYING SCOTSMAN CROSSING THE ROYAL BORDER BRIDGE, BERWICK-ON-TWEED

←Robert Stephenson's 1850 Royal Border Bridge at Berwick is one of the great markers on the East Coast route to Scotland. Its 28 elegant stone arches curve across the Tweed. This 1930s card shows the Flying Scotsman crossing.

↓This famous sequence of stone bridges spans the cutting that took the railway through Heckmondwike. Today, the railway has gone, and the bridges now cross an urban walkway and cycle track.

The Viaduct from Bridge, Bishop Auckland.

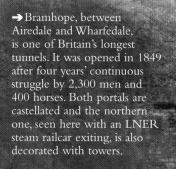

↑An Edwardian postcard view of Newton Cap viaduct shows its tall stone arches crossing the Wear. Opened in 1856 and closed in 1968, it was carefully adapted in 1995 to carry the A689 road.

➜Bramhope, between Airedale and Wharfedale, is one of Britain's longest tunnels. It was opened in 1849 after four years' continuous struggle by 2,300 men and 400 horses. Both portals are castellated and the northern one, seen here with an LNER steam railcar exiting, is also decorated with towers.

GOODS TRAINS

The North of England was the birthplace of modern railways, and the inspiration for most of the early lines was the need to find better ways to move minerals such as coal and stone. By the 1830s primitive locomotives hauling long lines of loaded wagons were a common sight, particularly in the Northeast. From these beginnings a vast railway network was developed through the 19th century, dedicated largely to the transport of freight to serve industry and for the export trade. This pattern was maintained through much of the 20th century, despite the increasing importance of passenger transport. Today the emphasis is on the movement of bulk cargoes and the international container traffic.

← Coal was always a primary cargo, with much of it going to the docks for export. By the 1960s, when this photograph was taken, power stations were the major coal users: in evening light, a Black Five hauls its coal train towards Stalybridge power station.

↓ In May 1965 steam-hauled freight was still a common sight in the North. Here, near Oxenholme, two former LMS locomotives, Class 5MT No. 45321 and, at the rear, Class 4MT No. 42095, share the burden of a mixed goods.

EX ROCKINGHAM COLLIERY

NEWTON, CHAMBERS & Co. Ld.

WASHED GAS NUTS

No. 2444 Date 6/5/22 Weight T. 8 C. 3

TO WHITBY (Gas Wks Sdg)
L. & N. E. (N. E. Section) RLY.
VIA DONCASTER

Consignee:- WHITBY GAS COMPANY

→ Until the pit closures of the 1980s, the transport of coal was the backbone of British Rail's freight business. Here, in the Warrington area, a heavily loaded coal train is hauled round a tight curve by a Class 47 diesel.

↓ Even the grandest of locomotives could be given freight duties. In the 1960s a streamlined Class A4, No. 60001, 'Sir Ronald Matthews', brings a southbound mixed freight past the former York excursion platform at Holgate.

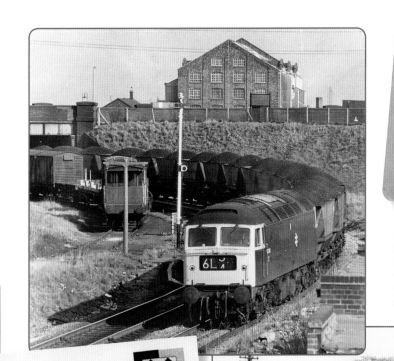

Date

Sender: National Coal Board
Durham Division No. 5 Area

From BRANDON COLLIERY—B.R.
PIT HOUSE WASHERY

TO Private Sidings,
HAVERTON HILL

Rly.   N E Section

Via

HB

Owner and   Weight   T   C
No. of Wagon

Description : PIT HOUSE
                    WASHED COKING SMALLS
Consignee IMPERIAL CHEMICAL INDUSTRIES LTD.
                    BILLINGHAM DIVISION

↓ Aycliffe signal box might be looking a bit past its best, but it is a sunny spring day and the windows are open as D5281 passes at the head of an up freight in the early 1970s.

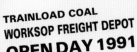

TRAINLOAD COAL
WORKSOP FREIGHT DEPOT
OPEN DAY 1991
£1

↘ In April 1967 a relatively new Brush Type 4 diesel, a member of a class of over 500 locomotives later more familiar as 47s, takes a car train across a misty Blea Moor while a steam-hauled mixed freight waits in the passing loop.

LOCOMOTIVE SHEDS

From the earliest days of the railways, the North of England boasted large and impressive engine sheds, thanks to the mixture of heavy freight traffic and mainline express passenger services that has always characterized the region. The challenging nature of the landscape and the frequently harsh weather made heavy demands on locomotives and their crews, so good maintenance was a priority. Sheds tended, as a result, to be large and well equipped. The steam age ended in northern England in 1968, and since then most of the famous sheds have been either closed or demolished, along with the coaling and water towers that were an essential feature of the railway scene for so many decades. A few sheds lived on as diesel motive power depots, albeit on a much reduced scale, but today only Carnforth survives to tell the tale.

⬇Carlisle Kingmoor was a famous name in northern locomotive sheds. Here, in 1965, A3 Class No. 60085, 'Manna', is on the turntable, while one of the depot's many Black Fives awaits its turn. The shed was closed on 31 December 1967.

➡Also famous was Hull Dairycoates shed. This 1928 photograph taken for the LNER magazine shows the wheel drop in use. A note on the back of the photo says the handrails, usually continuous for safety reasons, had been removed for the shot.

⬇This atmospheric view of Birkenhead shed in 1966 shows the reality of railway life on shed in the steam age, with the locomotive beneath the coaling tower hidden by clouds of smoke and steam.

↑Holbeck, near Leeds, boasted a classic roundhouse, seen here at the end of its active life. It is 1968 and only a couple of weeks before the end of steam on the British railway network. The four locomotives facing the turntable, a Jubilee, an 8F and a pair of 4MTs, will soon be on their last journey – to the scrapyard.

Thornaby TE

↑A mixed bag of locomotives await the scrapyard in Normanton shed sidings shortly before its closure. Two Victorian veterans head the queue, a former NER Class J72 tank and a 3F 0-6-0 from the Midland Railway.

➜Carnforth is today a famous survivor, the only mainline steam shed still fully equipped and operational. In 1967 it was still hard at work maintaining its wide range of allocated locomotives, but the diesels had begun to take over.

RAILWAY WORKS

The first dedicated railway works to be opened in Britain were in the North of England, notably the Stockton & Darlington Railway works at Shildon and those associated with the Stephensons in Newcastle, both of which started in the 1820s. Later, more famous names, including Darlington, Doncaster and Horwich, came into operation, all of which survived into the British Railways era. These were important centres of maintenance and overhaul, as well as locomotive building. Also important in the region were the numerous wagon building works. Many of these were established to cater for the increasing demand from private owners, particularly in the coal trade, during the latter part of the 19th century.

A few typical examples of RAILWAY WAGONS constructed by CHARLES ROBERTS & Co. Ltd. WAKEFIELD.

← A famous name in railway wagon building was Charles Roberts of Wakefield. This 1938 advertisement shows a typical range of products. Later, the company also built bodies for buses.

→ Doncaster works was set up by the Great Northern Railway in 1853, and continued to build steam locomotives into the 1950s. This photograph shows a workshop in the 1950s, with lathes and other tools used by apprentices and trainees.

↖ One of the many wagon building works in the North of England was at Faverdale, Darlington. This photograph from the LNER era shows the body-building shop for box vans. At that time it produced about 200 wagons a week.

← Horwich works was opened by the Lancashire & Yorkshire Railway in 1887. By 1958, when this photograph was taken, it was dedicated to repair and overhaul. In February of that year, this Class 1F tank, a Lancashire & Yorkshire veteran of 1897, was in pieces.

↑ Among the famous Doncaster-built locomotives are 'Flying Scotsman' and 'Mallard'. Steam locomotive building ceased at Doncaster in 1957, but the works was rebuilt as an important centre for the building and maintenance of diesel locomotives. This shows a pair of Class 55 Deltics in for overhaul.

↑ Darlington works opened in 1863 and locomotives were still being built in the mid-1950s. Here, two Class 2 British Railways Standards are under construction.

→ At Doncaster there were also important carriage and wagon building works. By the 1950s, when this was taken, maintenance was more important than building.

ALONG MAIN LINES
SCOTLAND

North Express crossing Forth Bridge.

London and North Eastern Railway
Express leaving Edinburgh.

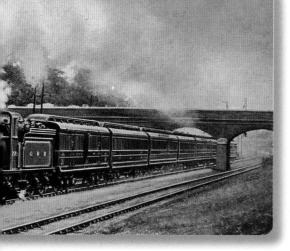

THE "FLYING SCOTSMAN" PASSING HADLEY WOODS.

BRITISH RAILWAYS. *LONDON MIDLAND REGION.* The UP Royal Scot train hauled by twin diesel-electric locomotives leaving Shrugboro' tunnel near Stafford. This bore was constructed to avoid disturbing the handsome

TRAIN SCENES

Thanks to its varied and often dramatic landscape and its distinctive railway history, Scotland holds a special appeal for the enthusiast and the photographer. As a result, Scottish railways have been well documented throughout the 20th century, with particular emphasis on the years of the LMS and LNER, and then British Railways. There are also plenty of modern images, for even today's bland and uniform trains can look good in Scotland's scenery.

→ The famous railway historian OS Nock took this photograph of the approach to the horseshoe bend on the West Highland line, a typically Scottish conjunction of great landscape and exciting engineering. In Scotland even railway enthusiasts can take a picture without a train in it.

↓ It would be hard to find a photograph with a greater sense of nostalgia than this 1930s image: a wayside garage, old cars, an AA man with his combination, a kilted passerby and a pair of former North British Railway K Class Glens heading a train near Tyndrum.

↓ Most railway signs were functional, but some were just decorative. This LNER border marker at Marshall Meadow, north of Berwick, combined elegance and symbolism. The network is less interesting without such things.

↑With steam on its way out in Scotland in 1965, there was still time to capture classic images. On a summer's Sunday evening an LNER Class V2, No. 60818, takes the train from Aberdeen to Glasgow via Dundee out of Montrose on the fine Ferryden viaduct running across the now filled-in Montrose Basin.

↓Another Scottish feature popular with photographers was the steep gradients and high summits. A favourite was Beattock Bank, and in August 1964 a holiday relief from Blackpool to Glasgow was storming up the bank, with a British Railways Standard Class 5, No. 73089, marking its efforts with plenty of smoke.

↑The challenge of harsh winters has always been a part of Scottish railway history, with many lines, particularly in the Highlands, regularly closed by snow. In December 1906 three locomotives were struggling to force the snowplough through the drifts at Auchterneed, on the Kyle of Lochalsh line.

←By 1965 the railway closure programme was having a massive impact, particularly in Scotland. This is clearly apparent in this view of a derelict-looking Pinmore station, where a relief train from Stranraer is passing through, headed by a pair of LMS Black Fives, No. 45486 and No. 45120.

↑Another double-header, this time a troop train from Woodburn to Stranraer via Dumfries, approaches Lochanhead in June 1965, days before the line closed. The locomotives are a Black Five, No. 45432, and a Standard Class 6P5F, No. 72007, 'Clan Mackintosh'.

↓Even famous locomotives had to take on ordinary duties. It is a bright day, after summer rain, and a smart-looking Class A4, No. 60034, 'Lord Faringdon', effortlessly hauls a long mixed goods away from the Forth bridge.

↘ Double-heading was a regular sight on many Scottish routes, including the lines to Stranraer. This is an excursion returning to Glasgow, near Maybole in 1963. Black Fives were often the favoured locomotives because of their power and reliability. This pair is No. 45460 and No. 44719.

↓ Local pick-up goods trains were an important part of mainline freight business, and this is how many of the wagons started and ended their journeys. Here, in June 1958, No. 57451, a veteran of former Caledonian Railway Class 2F – a design dating back to 1883 – hauls a typical mixed bag along near Thankerton, in open Scottish lowland scenery.

↑ This official LNER 1937 photograph of the Flying Scotsman crossing the border near Berwick, on the East Coast main line, was issued to celebrate the then-new streamlined A4 locomotives. This is No. 4492, 'Dominion of New Zealand'. The pair to the Scotland–England border marker is shown on page 212.

↑Another favourite place has always been Kyle of Lochalsh, the terminus of the Highland Railway's Skye line, completed in 1897. In this typically busy scene, probably from the 1950s, a train is ready to depart, a ferry sits by the dock, the goods lines are at work and a coach waits to take passengers on a tour of the Highlands.

↑Class 55 Deltic diesel locomotives made their mark on the East Coast main line, but visits to other parts of the Scottish network were much less frequent. In August 1972 No. 55017, 'The Durham Light Infantry', tours the Clyde Valley line while on a diversion.

➔Another early diesel type well known in Scotland was the Class 45, more popularly known as the Peaks. This is No. 45022, 'Lytham St Annes', taking the up Thames Clyde Express through Drumlanrig Gorge in July 1970.

↗ A passenger train winds its way into Edinburgh on a misty day in the early 1980s. The locomotive is a Class 26, a type introduced from 1961 and particularly associated with Scottish routes in the latter part of their service life.

↘ Finally, Scotland's most familiar diesel locomotive, the Class 37, takes a London-bound express past Garrochburn signal box, on the Nith Valley line, in 1963.

AT THE STATION

Scotland's earliest railways were industrial lines, usually linked to coal, but passenger services became important with the opening of the Edinburgh & Glasgow Railway in 1842. From that point the network grew steadily, reaching Aberdeen by 1850 and Inverness by 1863. By 1900 every town of substance in Scotland had a railway connection, despite the challenges posed by landscape and weather. At the same time, important suburban and industrial networks were developed, along with ever-expanding tourist traffic. This diversity resulted in a great variety of stations, from major city termini to those serving local lines. In many cases, the architecture reflected the grand ambitions of their original builders.

➜ One of the world's great railway views is Edinburgh's Waverley station, set in the valley between the Old and New towns. It all started in 1847, when three separate stations were built, but the scene here, with the station flanked by hotels, is the result of a redevelopment programme that was completed in 1900.

↘ Following its naming ceremony and looking immaculate in the original two-tone green livery, Class 55 Deltic No. D9000, 'Royal Scots Grey', departs from Edinburgh on 18 June 1962 for the centenary run of the Flying Scotsman.

◄⬇The second great station in Edinburgh was Princes Street, built by the Caledonian Railway from 1870. It was closed in 1965 and subsequently demolished. These two 1940s photographs show the spacious concourse, the island booking office, the clock tower and the decorative panelling, all of which dated from the 1890s.

⬆ Edinburgh Waverley aroused mixed feelings from the start, with many believing that the station's dominant position damaged the city. However, there were always plenty of postcards, such as this Edwardian example, which features the station with the North British Hotel.

➡ This 1960 view shows a train preparing to leave Glasgow's St Enoch station. Opened in 1876, it was used largely by the Glasgow & South Western Railway, which later became part of the LMS. Closed in 1966, it was demolished in 1977, along with its accompanying hotel.

← In the 1920s, Gourock was a thriving Clydeside resort, thanks in part to the Caledonian Railway's station and pier, which opened in 1889. Here, passengers could step straight from the platform onto Clyde steamers. The grand style of the station reflects the importance of Clyde tourist traffic to the railway companies.

↑ Opened in 1883 as part of an expansion of lines in the St Andrews and Leuchars area, Crail was closed in 1965. Here, in 1960, a local train, featuring the typical mix of carriages then found on lesser lines, is ready to depart.

↙↓ The last major lines to be built in Scotland were those serving Kyle of Lochalsh and Mallaig, the latter completed in 1901. Here, a special headed by Class 5 No. 44978 waits to depart from Kyle in 1962. while on the Mallaig line (below) a snow-covered Ben Nevis forms the backdrop for Banavie station.

The Highland Railway rebuilt Nairn station in 1885 in a decorative stone style. Here, in the 1950s, the signalman is using the official bicycle to ride between the timber signal cabins at each end of the platform. This unusual system stayed in use until 2000.

In an image of Inverness station that clearly shows its sharply curving platforms, two trains stand ready to depart one cold day in October 1970. Steam from the heating system rises from one locomotive, while the duffle-coated driver strides towards the other.

Inverness station, seen here in the 1980s, was the headquarters of the Highland Railway. It opened in 1862, a covered train shed at the apex of a triangle of lines that enclosed the railway works.

⬆ Two passengers wait for an early morning train at Dunkeld & Birnam station, on the line from Inverness to Perth. The elaborate Tudor-style stone station of 1856 was for a brief period the terminus of the Perth & Dunkeld Railway, before the route northwards was completed by the Inverness & Perth Junction Railway.

⬊ The complexity of Perth station, built and operated at the start by four companies, is apparent in a modern photograph. On the left, the western side, is the original station of 1848, with buildings by Sir William Tite. Later came the large central train shed. On the right are the curving platforms for the lines to Dundee, originally built as a terminus at right angles to the main station.

⬆ Beneath the delicate ironwork covering the western concourse at Perth, a girl with brightly coloured luggage hurries along an empty platform to catch her train. To the right is part of the original screen wall, rich with decorative stone details.

↑ This busy scene is Edinburgh Waverley on a summer's day in 2010. Set in the natural valley that divides the city, the station is approached via sloping ramps from street level. Much of the concourse, including the former booking office with its famous domed glass ceiling, is to the right of the ramp.

←↑ Waverley is both a terminus and a through station, with platforms at both ends. The station today is the legacy of the Victorian reconstruction programme, which created 19 full-length platforms underneath a vast glazed roof.

223

FAMOUS PLACES

THE FORTH BRIDGE

Familiar from countless postcards and souvenirs, and featured in many novels and films, not least in the various versions of *The Thirty Nine Steps*, the Forth bridge is probably Britain's most iconic railway structure. When opened by the Prince of Wales in March 1890, after five years of construction work, it was seen as one of the wonders of the world and revolutionary in terms of bridge building. The designer,

Sir Benjamin Baker, wisely abandoned earlier ideas for a suspension bridge, adopting the cantilever principle and using structural steel on an unprecedented scale. Postcards like the one on the left frequently listed the bridge's impressive statistics, but never mentioned the 57 deaths that occurred during construction.

Opened March 1890.
Height: 361 feet Length: 8296 feet
Spans: 1710 feet. Steel used: 54,160 tons.
Cost over £3,000,000.

FORTH BRIDGE FROM NORTH

⬇ The sheer sense of scale, and the complex patterns of steel tubes and latticework, have made the bridge enduringly popular with photographers. There are many versions of this classic image of an express pounding through the steelwork, but the combination of a streamlined A4 Pacific and this Victorian engineering masterpiece does take some beating.

→↓The size of the bridge dwarfs the trains that cross it, so photographs and postcards often focus on the defining characteristics of the bridge itself. The 1935 example (right) shows originality, if nothing else. The centenary in March 1990 (below right) was widely celebrated.

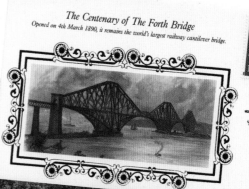

1990 R2

The Centenary of The Forth Bridge

Opened on 4th March 1890, it remains the world's largest railway cantilever bridge.

1890   1990

4 MAR 1990

SOUTH QUEENSFERRY W. LOTHIAN

Benham
The Bayle,
Folkestone

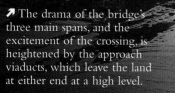

↗ The drama of the bridge's three main spans, and the excitement of the crossing, is heightened by the approach viaducts, which leave the land at either end at a high level.

TUNNELS, BRIDGES & VIADUCTS

The demanding nature of the landscape has ensured that Scotland has some of Britain's most dramatic, and most famous bridges and viaducts. Many are striking memorials to the ambitions of railway builders in the region, combining structural efficiency with architectural elegance. The greatest of these, for example the Forth and Tay bridges, were astonishing achievements when first completed. Even the collapse of the latter advanced the science of railway engineering. There are plenty of tunnels but, despite the Highland landscape, none are longer than the longest tunnels south of the border.

➜ Moncrieff tunnel, south of Perth, was completed by the Scottish Central Railway in 1848. By 1900 the rock lining was in a dangerous state, so the tunnel was lined with brick. This shows the concrete plant at the north entrance during the four-year rebuilding project.

↘ In July 1963 Coronation Class No. 46320, 'Duchess of Buccleuch', hauls its train out of Drumlanrig tunnel. Over 4,000ft long, the tunnel was built by the Glasgow & South Western Railway for their route to Carlisle via Kilmarnock.

BRITISH RAILWAYS. *SCOTTISH REGION.* An A2 class mixed traffic locomotive hauling a freight train across the Tay Bridge. This famous structure, over two miles long and having 85 spans was opened in 1887. The piers of the ill-fated earlier bridge can still be seen.

← The Tay bridge has featured in many postcards over the years. This example, with explanatory caption, was posted in 1951.

↓ The Findhorn viaduct, completed in 1897, crosses the river valley near Tomatin, Its nine iron lattice spans are supported on stone piers.

FINDHORN VIADUCT, TOMATIN   838

↓ Glenfinnan is the most famous viaduct on the West Highland Railway's line to Mallaig, both for its setting and its pioneering use of concrete for its 21 arches. This 1980s photograph, taken as a Mallaig-bound special crosses, headed by a Class 37 diesel, shows the magnificent balance of landscape and structure.

↘ In April 1962 a train crosses the Ballochmyle viaduct near Mauchline, in southwest Scotland. When the viaduct was completed in 1848, its main arch was the world's largest masonry span. It is still, at 169ft, the highest railway viaduct in Britain.

GOODS TRAINS

Dramatic scenery and a complex network linking major towns and cities with some of the most remote corners of the country gave a distinctive quality to Scotland's railways. Goods traffic was always important, on the one hand serving the major industries such as coal, engineering, ship building and fishing, and on the other being a vital source of trade and supplies for agriculture, the military and rural life. Until the latter part of the 20th century, large areas of Scotland were dependent on the railways for the maintenance of daily life.

→ Weather and landscape always make great demands on those maintaining Scotland's network. Here, in July 1975, a ballast train working on track maintenance pauses at Rannoch. Pretty in summer, this remote station on the Fort William line is often cut off in winter. In charge is a Class 24 diesel, No. 24104. Introduced in 1958, these locomotives were all withdrawn by 1980.

↓ In evening light, the regular mixed goods for Dundee crosses the river Tay as it curves away from Perth General station. It is the mid-1960s, and steam is on the way out in Scotland, making the old Class B1 locomotive an increasingly rare sight.

L.N.E.R.

SHUNT WITH GREAT CARE. LOAD and UNLOAD OUTSIDE GOODS SHEDS.

↑ A worn-looking Stanier Class 5MT, No. 44763, drifts down past Harthope, on Beattock Bank, with a southbound mixed goods in 1963. The crew have some time to relax and enjoy the view, probably well deserved after working the locomotive up the demanding gradient.

↑ Another photograph from the last years of steam in Scotland shows a smart Class A2 locomotive, No. 60527, 'Sun Chariot', at the head of the regular Perth-to-Aberdeen mixed goods. The location is near Luncarty, south of Stanley Junction, so the driver, watching the road, has a long journey ahead.

← In April 1961 an up tanker train passes Beattock Summit, headed by an old Class 5MT Crab, No. 42746. With the summit passed, the fireman has time to look out of the cab and watch the photographer.

LOCOMOTIVE SHEDS

The Scottish railway network, much of it in a demanding landscape that taxed locomotives to their limit, included busy freight and industrial lines, long-distance passenger services, and suburban and holiday routes.

The companies who built the network, notably the North British, the Caledonian, the Highland and the Glasgow & South Western, constructed a great variety of sheds to maintain the locomotives that operated it, some of which are represented here. The majority of Scotland's locomotive sheds have been lost since the closures of the 1960s, including such architectural masterpieces as the classic roundhouse at Inverness. A rare survivor, however, is Ferryhill.

← During the 1950s an elderly Class J35 locomotive, No. 64492, waits on the turntable at Dundee Tay Bridge shed. The class was designed for the North British Railway, with the first member being built in 1906.

↑ The most exciting shed in Scotland was the Highland Railway's roundhouse at Inverness, a classic example of the type, with 31 locomotive stalls connected to a central turntable. Shown here early in the 20th century, it was demolished in the 1960s.

→ This view of Inverness, probably in the late 1950s, shows the curve of the roundhouse on the left and the castellated water tower in the centre, both famous Highland Railway structures now demolished. Black Fives wait by the coaling tower.

← The most common type of shed was the linear variety, with locomotives stored on parallel tracks. This shows a typical example at Dumfries, towards the end of its life. Built originally by the Glasgow & South Western Railway, it was demolished after closure in 1966.

→ Greenock Ladyburn shed was built by the Glasgow, Paisley & Greenock Railway. Its mixed stock of locomotives included small tanks for dock and industrial duties. This photograph was taken not long before closure in the 1960s. The shed was later demolished.

↓ The Caledonian Railway's Ferryhill shed served a wide range of traffic in the Aberdeen region. The buildings, which a railway trust aims to restore as a heritage centre, are seen here probably in the 1930s.

RAILWAY WORKS

With heavy engineering and ship building long established in the Glasgow region, it is not surprising that the city's association with locomotive and railway vehicle manufacturing started in the 1840s. From that date, a number of works were developed in the Springburn area, including Cowlairs and St Rollox. Not far away were the independent locomotive builders Neilson and Sharp Stewart, who amalgamated to form the North British Locomotive Company in 1903. There were railway works in other areas of Scotland, notably the Highland Railway's, in Inverness, and Inverurie, built by the Great North of Scotland Railway, but Glasgow was to remain the centre of the industry. Today, most of the big names have gone, but St Rollox lives on.

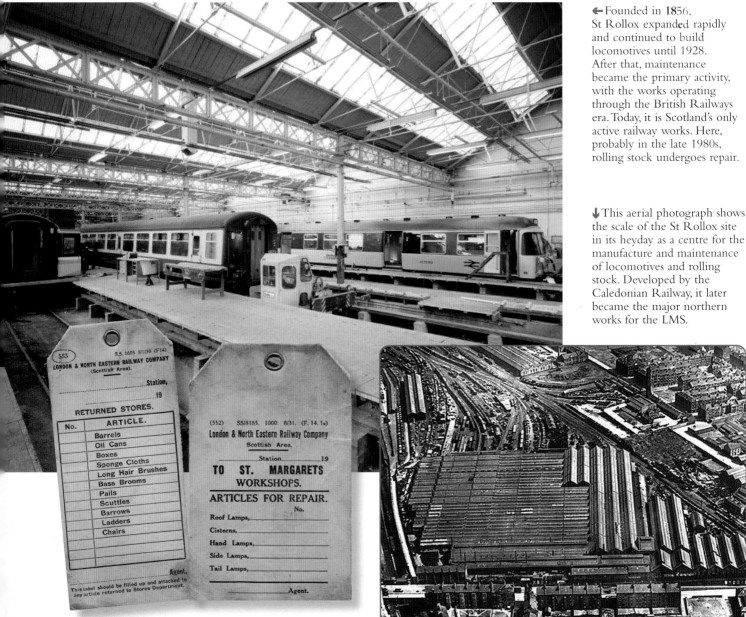

← Founded in 1856, St Rollox expanded rapidly and continued to build locomotives until 1928. After that, maintenance became the primary activity, with the works operating through the British Railways era. Today, it is Scotland's only active railway works. Here, probably in the late 1980s, rolling stock undergoes repair.

↓ This aerial photograph shows the scale of the St Rollox site in its heyday as a centre for the manufacture and maintenance of locomotives and rolling stock. Developed by the Caledonian Railway, it later became the major northern works for the LMS.

↑ These labels from the LNER's Scottish region are a reminder that railway maintenance went far beyond locomotives and rolling stock.

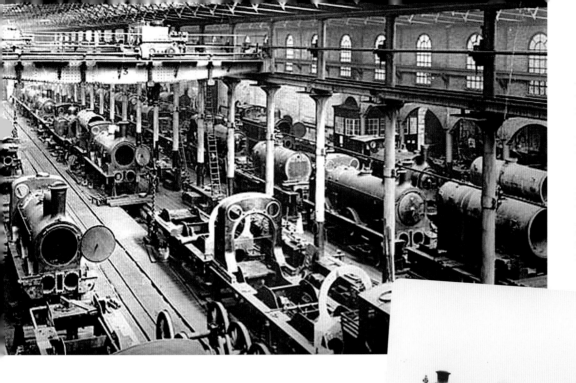

Glasgow's first railway works was Cowlairs, opened in 1841 by the Edinburgh & Glasgow Railway and taken over later by the North British Railway. The first in Britain to build locomotives, wagons and carriages on the same site, it survived LNER and British Railways ownership, closing in 1968. Here, the lines of NBR locomotives under construction show the scale of manufacturing in the early 20th century.

The Great North of Scotland Railway opened its works at Inverurie, near Aberdeen, in 1903. Few locomotives were built, but it was a major maintenance facility until it closed in 1968. In the 1950s, a former North British Class J37 gleams after a major overhaul.

It was a tradition at most works to photograph every completed locomotive as it came out of the paint shop, and St Rollox was no different. Some were photographed in primer, but the brand new McIntosh 4-4-0 shown here is ready for Caledonian service.

LOST MAIN LINES

ACROSS THE NETWORK

Dr Richard Beeching's 1963 report, *The Reshaping of British Railways*, recommended the closure of over 2,000 stations and thousands of miles of railway. The next few years saw the railway map of Britain radically redrawn. Cuts and closures across the nation primarily affected branch lines and rural routes, no longer viable because of changing traffic patterns and the impact of road transport. However, there were some significant mainline closures, including the former Great Central Railway's line to the Midlands and the North (see pages 242–51), the Somerset & Dorset Joint Railway, the Waverley route in Scotland and the old Southern Railway network in Devon and Cornwall. Also lost were many subsidiary lines that, although primarily country railways, served as important feeder and connecting lines and freight routes.

➜ One of England's most complicated scheduled services was the Atlantic Coast Express, linking London Waterloo with destinations in Devon and Cornwall. A popular holiday route, it was a lifeline for resorts like Ilfracombe, which was served by a short branch from Barnstaple. Seen here in 1973, after closure, is the old iron viaduct that took the line over the river at Barnstaple and northwards to Ilfracombe.

↘ Much of the old LSWR North Cornwall line has vanished, but the route can be traced and plenty survives to be discovered in the countryside. This bridge is hidden in woods near the junction with the Wadebridge-to-Bodmin line.

← Most closed railways were simply abandoned in the landscape. Others were given a new life as footpaths or cycle ways. This is Bideford, whose grand station and platforms survive, now flanking a popular cycle route.

↓ When a line was closed, much of the infrastructure was removed, including iron bridges, which had a significant scrap value. Survivals were, therefore, both rare and apparently random. At Fremington the viaduct over the estuary was spared, to be enjoyed in later years by walkers and cyclists.

↑ It is surprising how relics can linger on. In the 1990s the remains of a Southern Railway cast-iron warning sign was still standing in the wilderness around Holsworthy station.

↖ Many Beeching closures reflected the line duplication created by company rivalries. Barnstaple, for example, was served by the GWR and the LSWR. Despite being an important freight link, the GWR line from Taunton closed. There are plenty of relics along the route.

← A major mainline loss was the Somerset & Dorset line from the Midlands to the south coast via Bristol and Bath. As elsewhere, careful exploration can be rewarding. This embankment is near Bruton.

→ There were no significant mainline closures in Southeast England, but a number of important connecting and alternative routes were lost. Typical was the line from Guildford to Brighton via Horsham and Shoreham, where surviving structures made possible its reopening as a footpath and cycle way.

↑ The loss of the M&GN network, as well as other Norfolk lines, left the county with very few railways. Many traces can be seen in the landscape. This is a typical sight near Sedgeford, on the line from Heacham to Wells-next-the-Sea.

→ Another important cross-country link in East Anglia was the line from Cambridge to Colchester via Sudbury, a vital freight route during World War II. This is Clare station, a famous survival, but lesser-known parts of the route can also be investigated.

A significant mainline loss in the North of England was the cross-Pennine route from Darlington to Penrith, and its continuation to Cockermouth and Workington. Dramatic engineering and magnificent scenery are a powerful combination, and much remains to be seen and enjoyed. Typical is this stretch of trackbed near Threlkeld, beneath a snow-capped Saddleback.

→ Wales suffered badly under Beeching, losing many cross-country and connecting routes. The resort of Porthcawl was served by a short branch, but it carried heavy holiday traffic. As so often happened at that time, the loss of the railway signalled the decline of the resort. This is the platform at Porthcawl Golfers Halt, now serving a muddy track.

← Luck and careful searching could, until recently, reveal unexpected relics on old railway routes. This North Eastern Railway boundary marker was spotted near Lartington, on the Darlington-to-Penrith via Stainmore route.

↑There were a number of important mainline losses in Scotland, not least the direct route to Stranraer and Portpatrick from Dumfries, via Castle Douglas and Newton Stewart. This is another line worth exploring, with plenty still to be found, including the remains of the Piltanton viaduct on the Portpatrick branch. This was partially blown up and then left to decorate the landscape.

→Killin Junction was on the line from Dunblane to Crianlarich, the old Callander and Oban route. Today, the remains of the platform survive, along with the trackbed, now providing a magnificent walk through glorious country. In the distance, the route of the Killin and Loch Tay branch can be seen dropping away to the left.

THE GREAT CENTRAL

In late Victorian Britain, the Manchester, Sheffield & Lincolnshire Railway was an important and ambitious company with routes all over the North of England. In 1893 ambition led it to gain Parliamentary approval for a London extension. Work started in 1895, and the 92-mile route opened fully in 1899, by which time the company had renamed itself the Great Central Railway. Built for high-speed running and generously engineered, the Great Central was Britain's last new main line until the completion of the Channel Tunnel link. The line's massive construction costs and the many established competitors for its major routes meant that the Great Central always faced an uphill struggle. It was destined to be short-lived, with express traffic ceasing in 1960 and closure following in 1966.

← The Great Central was popular with postcard publishers during the Edwardian era. Here, a Sheffield and Manchester express waits to depart from Marylebone, the Great Central's London terminus.

↓ In the 1930s an LNER Marylebone-to-Immingham boat train makes its way out of London, double-headed by two former Great Central locomotives, a Class C4 and a Class 1, both designed by John G Robinson.

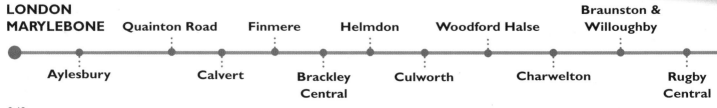

LONDON MARYLEBONE		Quainton Road		Finmere		Helmdon		Woodford Halse		Braunston & Willoughby	
	Aylesbury		Calvert		Brackley Central		Culworth		Charwelton		Rugby Central

➜ Marylebone was fronted by the Hotel Great Central, opened in 1899, complete with 700 bedrooms, a winter garden and a rooftop cycle track.

LIVERPOOL
OFFICIAL
ABC
TIME TABLE
GREAT CENTRAL RAILWAY
OCTOBER 1903
COLLECT ENCLOSED
PRIZE COUPONS SEE PARTICULARS OFFERED
PAGE 2 BY THE OFFICIAL PUBLISHERS

GOODS DEPOT.
GREAT CENTRAL RAILWAY.
MARYLEBONE

🖌 Much of the company's revenue came from goods traffic, particularly coal, and its fast running gave it an advantage over its rivals. Large goods depots were built at all major stations.

⬆ Marylebone was, by London standards, a modest mainline terminus, with Flemish-style detailing in brick and attractive ironwork. The hotel was altogether much grander.

GREAT CENTRAL RY.
DRAY TO CALL.

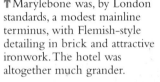

⬅ Another Edwardian card shows a classic view of a Great Central express leaving Marylebone, hauled by a typical Robinson-designed, green-painted C4 Class GCR 4-4-2 locomotive.

⬆ The Great Central's new main line ran from Annesley Junction, north of Nottingham, to Quainton Road in rural Buckinghamshire, where it joined the existing Metropolitan Railway network.

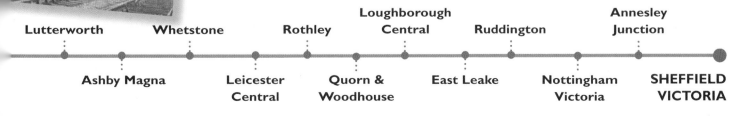

Lutterworth   Whetstone   Rothley   Loughborough Central   Ruddington   Annesley Junction

Ashby Magna   Leicester Central   Quorn & Woodhouse   East Leake   Nottingham Victoria   SHEFFIELD VICTORIA

↗➡ Today, much of the railway's route can be traced in the landscape and many of the structures survive. Great Central stations were generally built in brick to a standard design, with a large island platform. Calvert, in Buckinghamshire, is a typical example. The platforms and bridges survive, though all the buildings have gone. This section of the route is still used by freight trains.

↑➡ Many towns and villages gained a much better service with the coming of the Great Central, with Brackley, also in Buckinghamshire, being a notable example. These two photographs show Brackley Central looking rural in the 1950s, by which time the great days of the GCR had passed. On the right, enthusiasts wander around the platforms, and there is time to photograph a little boy in a rather dangerous spot.

(G. W. C. 60.)

**G. W. & G. C. RLYS.
JOINT COMMITTEE.**

Woodford

The arrival of the Great Central turned Woodford Halse, in Northamptonshire, into a railway town with an important junction and large locomotive sheds. Now, this massive cutting, inhabited by cows, and the bridge from which it was photographed, are the visible reminders of this railway past.

A Great Central locomotive brings a train into Woodford Halse, probably in the 1920s. In a typical reflection of the GCR's ambitions, the name board lists Dover and Folkestone as connections.

The Great Central's generous engineering, with deep cuttings excavated by steam-powered machinery and imposing bridges built in hard blue brick, has left its imprint in many places. This is near Helmdon, Northamptonshire. Some of the route may reopen as part of HS2, the planned high-speed line from London to Birmingham and beyond.

**WOODFORD
JUNCTION FOR
THE GREAT WESTERN RAILWAY**

DOVER FOLKESTONE AND STRATFORD

↗ Exploring the route produces many surprises. Here, Pink Floyd's fame lives on as graffiti on the abutment of a former GCR bridge over the canal near Braunston, Northamptonshire.

↓ Some sections of the line have completely vanished, but in many areas the route is still obvious in the landscape. This embankment and elegant bridge are near Wolfhampcote, Warwickshire.

↘ In a region rich with canal and railway history, the Great Central's broad embankments stride across the fields, revealing the company's determination to have fast-running trains throughout the route.

↓Another town given a new lease of life was Lutterworth. It is hard to believe that the overgrown remains of the station once witnessed the passage of expresses bound for Manchester and Sheffield.

↑In towns and cities with established railway routes, the Great Central had to make its own way, often at huge cost. This is Rugby Central, and the end is in sight as grass grows through the tracks and a battered old LMS Class 5MT takes water.

↘ Great earthworks such as viaducts and cuttings are enduring and will probably remain for hundreds of years. Bridges are less predictable as many of the metal ones were removed for scrap when the line was demolished. Some, randomly, remain.

G. W. R.

Rugby
(CENTRAL)
Via Banbury & G. C. Rly.

BRITISH RAILWAYS

ENGINEERING WORK
between
WOODFORD HALSE
and
LUTTERWORTH
on
SUNDAYS 27th JANUARY to
14th APRIL 1957

TRAIN SERVICE
ALTERATIONS

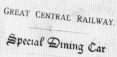

GREAT CENTRAL RAILWAY.

Special Dining Car

CRICKET MATCH.

LANCASHIRE
v.
YORKSHIRE,

Bramall Lane, Sheffield,
August 7th, 1905.

➜⬆East Leake, in Nottinghamshire, was a standard Great Central small station featuring the familiar style of brick buildings. It was set on an embankment with a road below. Today, overgrown platforms and battered fencing remain to be examined, on a section that is still used by freight trains.

⬇A large viaduct, built from the engineering brick favoured by the Great Central, spans the valley of the Soar, near Stanford-on-Soar, on the Nottinghamshire/Leicestershire border. It may lack the elegance of Victorian viaducts, but it has a powerful presence. Freight trains still cross it.

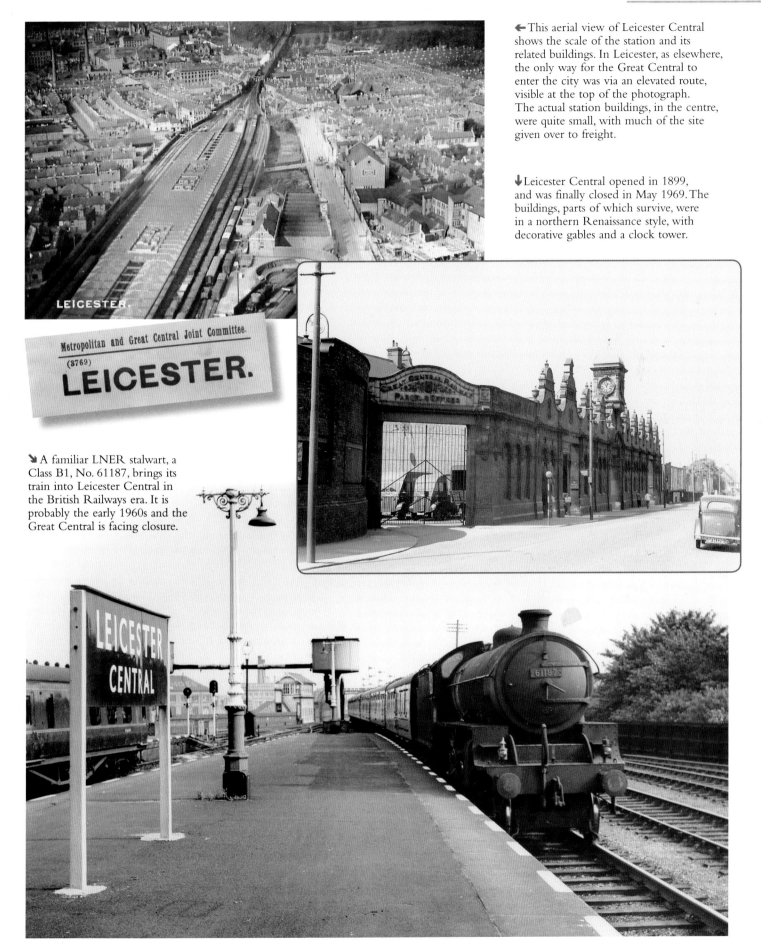

← This aerial view of Leicester Central shows the scale of the station and its related buildings. In Leicester, as elsewhere, the only way for the Great Central to enter the city was via an elevated route, visible at the top of the photograph. The actual station buildings, in the centre, were quite small, with much of the site given over to freight.

↓ Leicester Central opened in 1899, and was finally closed in May 1969. The buildings, parts of which survive, were in a northern Renaissance style, with decorative gables and a clock tower.

LEICESTER.

Metropolitan and Great Central Joint Committee.
(8769)
LEICESTER.

↘ A familiar LNER stalwart, a Class B1, No. 61187, brings its train into Leicester Central in the British Railways era. It is probably the early 1960s and the Great Central is facing closure.

➜ Nottingham boasted four main stations, the last being Victoria, opened by the Great Central in 1900 and seen here in the late 1940s. It is the early days of British Railways, but LNER signs are still apparent. The photograph does not show the decorative stonework at its best.

↓ By contrast, this card shows the recently completed station and hotel in full glory, a rich assembly of French Renaissance styling in Derbyshire stone and red brick. After closure in 1967, all but the clock tower was swept away.

Victoria Station and Hotel, Nottingham.

1201. 3.

Woodhead Tunnel, Great Central Ry.

The Wrench Series No. 4541

↓ Sheffield's Victoria station, opened in 1851, was redeveloped in 1908 to suit the needs of the Great Central. At the same time, it acquired its typical clock tower. Busy until the 1960s, the station closed in 1970 and was demolished in 1989.

↑ There were three tunnels at Woodhead, on the line from Manchester to Sheffield. The second, seen here with a Great Central train entering in about 1910, was opened in 1852 by the Manchester, Sheffield & Lincolnshire Railway, the Great Central's predecessor.

BRITISH RAILWAYS   VICTORIA STATION   BRITISH RAILWAYS

←On 3 September 1966 the last scheduled passenger service on the Great Central line, the 5.15pm from Nottingham to Marylebone, leaves Woodford Halse. The LMS Class 5MT No. 44984 wears a wreath.

↓Almost immediately a preservation group was formed to save some of the route. From these early, difficult beginnings came the new Great Central Railway, Britain's only double-track mainline heritage railway.

←The current route links Loughborough and Leicester, and there are plans to extend the line. Here, a rail-mounted crane helps rebuild Loughborough Central station.

↑The GCR prides itself as a fully fledged mainline railway, operating to that standard. Here, signalman Brian Barton records train movements at Quorn & Woodhouse.

251

INDEX

A

Aberbeeg 7, 137
Aberdare 139
'Aberdonian' 189
Abergavenny 131
Aberystwyth 126
Advanced Passenger Train 15
air services 52–3
'Alberta' 59, 196
Allan, Ian 60
'Alycidon' 195
American Special 25
Andrews, GT 195
'Argyll and Sutherland
    Highlander' 194, 198
Arriva Trains Wales 130
arrivals and departures boards
    37, 155
Ashford 117, 118, 119
'Ashley Grange' 69, 86
Ashley Hill 74
Atlantic Coast Express 37, 236
atmospheric railway 83
Auchterneed 213
Aycliffe 205
Aynho 143

B

Badminton 142
'Baglan Hall' 148
Baker, Sir Benjamin 224
Ballochmyle viaduct 227
Banavie 220
Bangor 128
bar cars 28, 30, 59
Bargoed 128
Barmouth 123
Barmouth bridge 132–3
Barnstaple 80, 236, 238
Bath 68, 89
Battledown viaduct 112
'Baynardo' 188
Baynards 98
Beattock Bank 213, 229
Beeching closures 236–41
Berkeley Road Junction 147
Bideford 237
Bincombe Bank 72, 87
Birkenhead 206
Birmingham New Street 153
Birmingham Snow Hill 7, 152
'The Black Watch' 197
blackout blinds 19
Blair Atholl 34
Blue Pullman 29, 58, 84,
    129, 152
boat trains 17, 57, 96, 127,
    178, 183, 242
Bolton 197
'Book Law' 195
Bournemouth 76
'Bourton Grange' 143
Box tunnel 8
BR see British Railways

Brackley 244
Bradford 189, 194
Bramhope 203
breakdown trains 47
Breydon swing-bridge 181
bridges
    central England 158, 245, 246
    eastern England 181
    northern England 202, 203
    Scotland 45, 224–5, 227
    southwest England 85, 236
    Wales 132–3, 135, 145
Brighton 117, 118
Brighton Belle 57, 95
Bristol 72, 76, 78, 79, 88
Bristol & Exeter Railway 80
Britannia bridge 134, 135
British Railways (BR) 21, 29,
    30, 31, 36, 39, 48, 49, 56, 58,
    60, 62, 173
    locomotives 15, 72, 89, 94,
    110, 122, 123, 126, 136,
    158, 162, 164, 165, 174,
    191, 192, 209, 213, 214
British Transport Hotels 62
Bromley South 97
'Broome Manor' 71
Brunel, Isambard Kingdom 78,
    82, 84, 85, 90, 104, 108, 159
'Bude' 14
buffet cars 31
Bulleid, Oliver 11, 14, 28, 98
'Bunsen' 190
Bushey 145

C

Caerphilly 139
Caledonian 61
Caledonian Hotel, Edinburgh 65
Caledonian Railway 24, 33,
    65, 215, 219, 220, 231, 232
Calvert 244
Cambrian Coast Express 7, 58,
    122, 123
Camden Bank 147
Cannon Street 105
Cannon Street Hotel 62
car transport services 7, 54–5
Cardiff 64, 126
Carlisle 196
Carlisle Kingmoor 206
Carmarthen 127, 139
Carnforth 59, 207
carriage interiors 16–23
carriage prints 21
Cefn viaduct 135
Charing Cross 105, 109
Charles Roberts & Co 208
Chelmsford 183
'Chepstow Castle' 82
Chester 122, 145
Chester & Holyhead Railway
    64, 122, 128, 134
Chirk 135

cinema carriages 18
'City of Truro' 99
'Clan Mackintosh' 214
Clapham Junction 110–11
Clare 174, 239
clay wagons 86
Clayton tunnel 113
club cars 18, 20
'Clun Castle' 143
coal hoists 163
coal trains 7, 87, 137, 160, 163,
    175, 204, 205
Cockett 127
Colchester 172, 185
College Wood viaduct 85
Collett, CB 13
'Comet' 173
Condor freight service 48, 50
container traffic see freight
    business; goods trains
Conwy 124
Cornish Riviera Express 56, 83
Coronation 10, 18
Coronation Scot 10, 20, 28, 61
Cowlairs 232, 233
Cowley Bridge Junction 75
Crail 220
Crewe 15, 152, 164, 165
Cricklewood 163
Cromer 175
Crumlin viaduct 135
Cubitt, William 112

D

Dainton Bank 68, 75
Danygraig 139
Darlington 191, 208, 209
Dawlish Warren 45, 82–3
Dempster Sideloader 50
departures and arrivals boards
    37, 155
Derby 150, 163, 164, 165
Devon Belle 18, 56, 95
Devonian 82
dining cars see restaurant cars
DMU units 80, 124, 153, 171
Dobson, John 194
'Dominion of New Zealand'
    215
Doncaster 14, 197, 208, 209
double-heading 70, 80, 100,
    191, 214, 215, 242
Dovey Junction 123
driver cabs 171
Drumlanrig Gorge 216
Drumlanrig tunnel 226
'Duchess of Buccleuch' 226
'Duchess of Hamilton' 124, 190
Dumfries 231
Dundee Tay Bridge shed 230
Dunkeld & Birnam 222
'The Durham Light Infantry'
    216
Dutton viaduct 158

E

'Earl of Powis' 70
East Leake 248
Eastern Counties Railway
    169, 184
Eastleigh 88, 117, 118, 119
Edinburgh & Glasgow
    Railway 218, 233
Edinburgh Princes Street 219
Edinburgh Waverley 6, 218,
    219, 223
'Edward Thompson' 169
electrification 47
Elizabethan 61, 193
Ely 170, 176
engineering 44–7
    see also bridges; tunnels;
    viaducts
engineering trains 182
English Electric 14
English, Welsh & Scottish
    Railway (EWS) 51
'Epsom' 105
Eurostar 107
Euston 8, 37, 41, 100, 101
Evercreech Junction 80
EWS (English, Welsh &
    Scottish Railway) 51
Exeter 81
Exmouth 88, 89, 95

F

'Falmouth' 143
Farrell, Terry 105, 109
Faverdale 208
Fenman 171
Ferryden viaduct 213
Ferryhill 231
Findhorn viaduct 227
First Great Western 56, 80
Fishguard 127
'Flying Scotsman' locomotive
    12, 203, 209
Flying Scotsman train 8, 26,
    61, 195, 215, 218
Folkestone 96
Forth bridge 45, 214, 224–5
freight business 48–51, 72
    see also goods trains
Freightliner 48, 51
Fremington 237
'Fringford Manor' 70
Frodsham viaduct 161
Frome 80

G

Garrochburn 217
Garsdale 188
Gasworks tunnel 99
Gatwick Express 111
GER see Great Eastern
    Railway
Gisburn tunnel 202
Glasgow 47, 219

Glasgow & South Western Railway 65, 219, 226, 231
Glasgow, Paisley & Greenock Railway 231
Gleneagles 65
Glenfinnan viaduct 227
Gloucester 149
Gloucester & Sharpness canal 158
GNR see Great Northern Railway
Golden Arrow 56, 57, 94
Golden Hind 56
Gooch, Daniel 90
goods depots 6, 41, 243
goods trains
  central England 160–1
  eastern England 182–3
  northern England 204–5
  Scotland 215, 228–9
  southern England 114–15
  southwest England 86–7
  Wales 136–7
Gourock 220
Grand Junction Railway 158
Grand Midland Hotel, St Pancras 102
'Granville Manor' 58
Great Central Railway 63, 100, 162, 163, 236, 242–51
Great Eastern Hotel, Liverpool Street 63
Great Eastern Hotel, Harwich 64
Great Eastern Railway (GER) 64, 178, 180, 184
Great Malvern 148
Great North of Scotland Railway 232, 233
Great Northern Railway (GNR) 12, 17, 24, 32, 168, 208
Great Southern & Western Railway 127
Great Western Railway (GWR) 20, 24, 25, 26, 27, 32, 41, 42, 48, 56, 62, 76, 80, 81, 84, 90–1, 122, 126, 127, 130, 238
  locomotives 11, 13, 58, 68, 69, 70, 71, 73, 77, 79, 80, 83, 84, 85, 86, 87, 123, 124, 126, 132, 136, 139, 142, 143, 148, 150, 152, 159, 160, 165
'The Green Howards' 192
Greenock Ladyburn 231
Gresley, Sir Nigel 11, 12, 26
Griddle Car 31
Grosvenor Bank 94
guide books 37, 42–3
Guildford 116
GWR see Great Western Railway

H
Hadley Wood tunnel 144
Harrison, Thomas 202
Harwich 64, 178, 182
Harwich Continental 29, 178
Hattersley tunnel 45
Hawkshaw, Sir John 105
Hayle 69
Headstone viaduct 156
Heathrow Express 108
Heckmondwike 203
Helmdon 245
Hemerdon Bank 70
Hereford 150, 154
'Heveningham Hall' 70
Highbridge 91
Highland Railway 216, 221, 230, 232
Hither Green 114
Holbeck 207
'Holland-America Line' 71
Holloway Bank 146
Holsworthy 237
Holyhead Hotel 64
home removal services 48
Hornsey 116
Horwich 209
Hotel Great Central, Marylebone 243
hotels 62–5, 102, 194, 243
HS2 245
HST 125 15, 80, 81, 83, 107, 125, 131, 165
Hull Dairycoates 206
Hunt, HA 151
'Hush Hush' (LNER 10000) 11

I
Intercity 15, 173, 180
Inverness 221, 230, 231, 232
Inverness & Perth Junction Railway 222
Inverurie 232, 233
Ipswich 173, 176, 180
Irish Mail 56, 58, 100

J, K
Jacomb, W 76
'Kenilworth' 191
Kentish Belle 96, 97
Killin Junction 241
Kilsby tunnel 7
'King Edward VII' 152
'King George IV' 84
'King George V' 13
'King George VI' 13, 61
'King Henry VII' 11
Kings Cross 8, 46, 99, 103, 107, 146
Kings Lynn 185
Kingsbridge 70
Kingswear 71
kitchen cars 25, 26

'Knight of the Thistle' 193
'Kolhapur' 188
Kyle of Lochalsh 213, 216, 220

L
Ladore Hotel, Derwentwater 63
'Lady Godiva' 6, 144
Laira 73, 88
Laisterdyke 189
'Lambton Castle' 168
Lampeter 129
Lancaster & Carlisle Railway 200
Lancaster & Yorkshire Railway 209
Lancing 119
Lartington 240
lavatories 17
Lavenham 171
LB&SC see London, Brighton & South Coast Railway
Leamington Spa 147, 154
'Leander' 145
Leeds 6, 199
Leek 151
Leicester 163, 249
lineside guides 42–3
Littleborough 191
Liverpool 64, 198
Liverpool Street 101, 108, 171
Llandudno Junction 124
'Llanstephan Castle' 68
LMS see London, Midland & Scottish Railway
LNER see London & North Eastern Railway
LNWR see London & North Western Railway
Locke, Joseph 158
locomotive sheds
  central England 162–3
  eastern England 184–5
  northern England 206–7
  Scotland 230–1 southern England 46, 101, 102, 104, 105, 116–17
  southwest England 76, 80, 88–9
  Wales 7, 138–9
locomotives
  1 Class 242
  1F Class 209
  2 Class 159
  2F Class 215
  3F Class 207
  4F Class 183
  4MT Class 150, 204, 207
  5 Class 220
  5MT Class 159, 162, 191, 201, 204, 229, 247, 251
  8F Class 71, 207
  9F Class 162, 192
  22 Class 74

  24 Class 228
  25 Class 161
  26 Class 217
  30 (Brush Type 2) Class 170
  31 (Brush Type 2) Class 183, 185
  33 Class (Cromptons) 111, 115
  37 Class 15, 125, 128, 137, 170, 185, 217, 227
  40 Class 59, 61, 201
  43 Class 15
  45 Class 149, 153, 193, 216
  46 Class 147, 153
  47 Class (Brush Type 4) 72, 75, 83, 103, 124, 162, 171, 182, 197, 205
  50 Class 15, 75, 147, 153, 201
  52 Class 73, 79, 87
  55 Class Deltic 6, 14, 103, 146, 175, 192, 193, 194, 195, 197, 209, 216, 218
  57 Class 130
  66 Class 51
  85 Class 153
  86 Class 15, 147, 158, 173
  87 Class 7, 193, 197
  222 Class 199
  315 Class 171
  2251 Class 159
  2800 Class 160
  4300 Class 79, 150
  7200 Class 87, 138
  A1 Class 12, 189, 191
  A2 Class 169, 229
  A3 Class 12, 103, 144, 195, 206
  A4 Class 205, 10, 60, 99, 144, 195, 214, 215, 224
  Austerity Class 98
  B1 Class 172, 174, 178, 228, 249
  B12 Class 169
  Battle of Britain Class 11, 115
  Black Five Class 128, 204, 206, 214, 215, 231
  Britannia Class 94
  Bulldog Class 143
  C4 Class 242, 243
  Castle Class 7, 68, 70, 82, 83, 126, 143
  Coronation Class 226
  Deltic Class see 55 Class Deltic
  Experiment Class 200
  G2 Class 198
  Grange Class 69, 86, 143
  Hall Class 68, 70, 148
  J20 Class 183
  J35 Class 230
  J37 Class 233
  J39 Class 189

J72 Class 207
Jubilee Class 59, 100, 145, 152, 188, 191, 196, 198, 207
K Class 212
King Arthur Class 115
King Class 13, 84, 152
L Class 97, 98, 100
L1 Class 76
Lord Nelson Class 14, 117
McIntosh Class 233
Manor Class 58, 70, 71, 123
Merchant Navy Class 11, 14, 56, 71, 95
Modified Hall Class 70, 161
N7 Class 101
N15 Class 97
Pacific Class 11, 12, 14, 95, 96, 103, 144, 169, 189, 191, 195, 205, 206, 229
Patriot Class 6, 50, 144, 145, 190, 196, 200
Prairie Class 77
Princess Coronation Class 13, 61, 124, 190
Princess Royal Class 13
Royal Scot Class 128, 196, 198
S15 Class 114
Sandringham Class 168
Schools Class 105
Standard Class 126, 174, 191, 214
Standard Class 2 209
Standard Class 4 94, 122, 123, 136
Standard Class 5 89, 110, 164, 213
U Class 89, 119
V Class 98
V2 Class 182, 213
Victorian Class 47, 116, 117
Warship Class 74, 78, 83, 91, 149
West Country Class 11, 14, 49, 57, 74, 87, 95, 96
Western Class 88, 91
see also individual entries for named trains and locomotives
London 100–9
    Cannon Street 105
    Charing Cross 105, 109
    Euston 8, 37, 41, 100, 101
    Kings Cross 8, 46, 99, 103, 107, 146
    Liverpool Street 101, 108, 171
    Marylebone 101, 242, 243
    Paddington 13, 41, 104, 108
    St Pancras 7, 102, 107
    Victoria 57, 94, 106
    Waterloo 106, 108, 109

London & Brighton Railway 113
London, Brighton & South Coast Railway (LB&SC) 110, 118, 119
    locomotives 118
'The London Irish Rifleman' 196
London, Midland & Scottish Railway (LMS) 10, 17, 18, 20, 27, 28, 34, 42, 48, 63, 100, 122, 164, 165, 188, 219
    locomotives 6, 10, 13, 50, 71, 100, 128, 152, 188, 191, 204, 214, 247
London & North Eastern Railway (LNER) 6, 10, 18, 19, 20, 25, 26, 33, 34, 39, 42, 44, 49, 188, 232
    locomotives 10, 11, 12, 99, 101, 103, 169, 172, 179, 183, 184, 188, 213, 242, 249
London & North Western Railway (LNWR) 16, 17, 24, 25, 35, 63, 100, 122, 165
    locomotives 159, 200
London & South Western Railway (LSWR) 76, 80, 106, 110, 112, 118, 236, 238
    locomotives 110, 114, 119
London, Tilbury & Southend Railway 173
'Lord Faringdon' 214
'Lord Rodney' 117
LSWR *see* London & South Western Railway
Loughborough 155, 251
lounge cars 18, 20, 28
'The Loyal Regiment' 198
luggage 40
Lutterworth 247
'Lytham St Annes' 216

M
'Magnificent' 149
mail trains 40, 41
Mallaig 220
'Mallard' 10, 209
Manchester, Sheffield & Lincolnshire Railway 242, 250
'Manna' 206
Manor House Hotel, Moretonhampstead 62
'Manorbier Castle' 11
March 169
Margate 98
Mark's Tey 169
Marylebone 101, 242, 243
Maunsell, Richard 14, 98
'Meld' 146
'Melton' 103

Melton Constable 174, 185
Menai bridges 135
Merchant Venturer 68
Metropolitan Railway Carriage and Wagon Company 164
Midland Counties Railway 124
Midland & Great Northern (M&GN) 181, 239
Midland Hotel, Manchester 64
Midland Hotel, Morecambe 9, 64
Midland Pullman 58
Midland Railway 24, 150, 155, 156, 159, 163, 165, 194, 199, 207
Miller's Dale tunnel 159
Moncrieff tunnel 226
Monsal Dale 156–7
Morecambe 9, 63
Motive Power Depots 162
Motorail 54–5

N
Nairn 221
named trains 56–61
Network South East 171
Newcastle-on-Tyne 8, 192, 194
Newport 122, 125, 130, 131, 134, 138
Newton Abbot 68, 74, 88
Newton Cap viaduct 203
Night Ferry 96
Nine Elms 118
No. 1 (4-2-2) 12, 168
Nock, OS 212
Normanton 207
North British Locomotive Company 232
North British Railway 212, 230, 233
North Devon Railway 80
North Eastern Railway 240
North Staffordshire Railway 151
North Western Hotel, Liverpool 64
Northchurch 159
Norwich (Norwich Thorpe) 168, 175, 177, 181, 185
Nottingham 63, 150, 250
'Novelty' 198

O
observation cars 18
Ocean Express 25, 26
Ocean Liner Express 57
'Odney Manor' 123
Old Colwyn 134
Old Oak Common 116
open days and weekends 118, 163
'Orient Line' 56, 95

Oswestry & Newtown Railway 129
Oxted viaduct 113

P
Paddington 13, 41, 104, 108
parcel services 40, 41
Parkeston Quay 178, 179
Parkeston Quay Hotel 179
Patricroft 198
Pencader 127
Pencoed 137
Penmaenmawr viaduct 8
Penzance 77
Perth 222, 228
Perth & Dunkeld Railway 222
Peterborough 168, 182
Peters, Ivo 71
picnic saloons 24
pilot locomotives 168
Piltanton viaduct 241
Pinmore 214
Plymouth 73
'Polar Star' 126
Porthcawl 240
postcard views 8–9, 24, 33, 66–7, 76, 82, 92–3, 96, 102, 103, 105, 120–1, 132, 133, 134, 135, 140, 145, 150, 157, 158, 159, 162, 166–7, 173, 180, 181, 186–7, 200, 203, 210–11, 224, 227, 242, 243, 250
'Princess Elizabeth' 13
promotional literature 16, 20, 22, 24, 25, 27, 29, 30, 32, 35, 36–7, 48, 49, 52, 60, 62, 96, 100, 178, 179
Pullman trains 2, 7, 18, 20, 29, 56, 58, 59, 84, 94, 95, 97, 129, 146, 152, 171, 179

Q, R
Quintinshull 61
Quorn & Woodhouse 251
Railway Air Services 52–3
Railway Chronicle Travelling Charts 42
railway works
    central England 164–5
    eastern England 184–5
    northern England 208–9
    Scotland 232–3
    southern England 118–19
    southwest England 90–1
    Wales 138–9
Rainhill 192
Rannoch 228
Reading 115
Relly Mill 189
restaurant cars 24–31, 169
'Rhose Wood Hall' 161
Rhyl 122, 128
Rhymney Railway 139

Roadrailer 50
Robertson, Henry 135
Robinson, John G 242
'Rodney' 75
route books *see* lineside guides
Royal Albert bridge 69, 85, 86
Royal Border bridge 203
royal carriages 16
The Royal Duchy 56
'Royal Lancer' 12
Royal Scot 18, 56, 61, 100, 128
'Royal Scots Grey' 218
Rugby 9, 164, 247

S

St Pancras 7, 102, 107
St Pancras Hotel 102
St Pinnock viaduct 85
St Rollox 232, 233
Saltash 69, 85
Saltley 162, 164
Sandringham Hotel, Hunstanton 64
Scarborough Flyer 60
Scotrail 34
Scottish Central Railway 226
'Seagull' 60, 195
season tickets 36
Selby 202
SER *see* South Eastern Railway
Severn tunnel 75, 136
Shakespeare Cliff tunnel 112
Shap Summit 50, 200–1
'Sharpshooter' 74
Shawford 99
sheds *see* locomotive sheds
Sheffield 197, 199, 250
Sheffield Pullman 146
Shepton Mallet viaduct 45
Shoeburyness 184
Shrewsbury 122, 162
Shrewsbury & Chester Railway 135
Silver Jubilee 10
'Sir Blamor de Ganis' 115
'Sir Frederick Harrison' 50
'Sir Nigel Gresley' 12, 99
'Sir Ronald Matthews' 205
sleeper trains 32–5, 96
smoking compartments 19
snowploughs 213
Somerset & Dorset Joint Railway 45, 71, 80, 89, 91, 236, 238
Somerton 73
'South Africa' 152
South Eastern Hotel, Deal 63
South Eastern Railway (SER) 96, 105, 112, 118
South Yorkshireman 59, 190
Southend 182

Southern Belle *see* Brighton Belle
Southern Railway 28, 37, 42, 109, 118, 236
    locomotives 11, 14, 76, 89, 97, 98, 117, 119
Speedfreight 48
'Spitfire' 115
Stanier, Sir William 10, 13
Starcross 83
Station Hotel, Fort William 65
stations
    central England 148–55
    eastern England 172–7
    northern England 194–9
    Scotland 218–23
    southwest England 76–81
    Wales 126–31
Stephenson, Robert 124, 134, 203
Stirling, Patrick 12, 168
Stockton & Darlington Railway 208
Stoke Gifford 2
Stoke-on-Trent 151
Stourbridge 143
Stratford (London) 184, 185
streamlining 10–11, 164
'Sun Chariot' 229
Sutton bridge 181
Swansea 125, 129
Swindon 90–1
swing-bridges 181, 202
'Swordfish' 7

T

Takeley 175
Talerddig Bank 122, 136
Taunton 80
Tavern Cars 30
'Tavistock' 95
Tay bridge 227
Tebay 190, 201
Teignmouth 87
Telford, Thomas 135
'Temeraire' 147
'Templecombe' 57
Templecombe (locomotive shed) 89
Tenby 137
Thanet Belle *see* Kentish Belle
Thompson, Francis 128, 150, 176
Threlkeld 240
ticket offices 36
ticket prices 36
timetables 38–9
Tite, Sir William 222
Toton 163
track maintenance 44, 47, 182
train scenes
    central England 142–7
    eastern England 168–71
    northern England 188–93

Scotland 212–17 southern England 94–9 southwest England 68–75 Wales 122–5
Tregenna Castle Hotel 62
'Trematon Castle' 126
Trowse Junction 170
Trowse swing-bridge 181
Truro 77
tunnels
    central England 7, 144, 159
    eastern England 180
    northern England 45, 202, 203, 250
    Scotland 226
    southern England 99, 112, 113
    southwest England 8, 75, 84
    Wales 125, 134, 136
turntables 71, 116, 163, 191, 206, 207, 230
Twerton 84
Tyne-Tees Pullman 59

U, V

Upminster 172
Upwey and Broadway 72
viaducts
    central England 156, 158, 161, 248
    northern England 203
    Scotland 213, 227, 241
    southern England 112, 113
    southwest England 45, 85, 237
    Wales 8, 134, 135
'Victoria' 191
Victoria (station) 57, 94, 106
Victoria Hotel, Nottingham 250
Virginia Water 114

W

Wadebridge 88
wagon building works 208
Waterhouse, Alfred 64
Waterloo 106, 108, 109
Watford tunnel 159
'The Welch Regiment' 128
Welcombe Hotel, Stratford-upon-Avon 63
Welshpool 129
Wenford Bridge 86
West Cornwall Railway 69
West Highland Railway 65, 212, 227
Westbury 87
Westcliff-on-Sea 173
'Western Nobleman' 87
'Western Sentinel' 73
'Whimple' 96
'Whitbourne Hall' 70
Whitchurch 149
White Rose 99

Whitemoor 6, 182, 183
Wickford Junction 173
Wigan 196
'William Shakespeare' 94
Wilson, Edward 101
Wolverhampton 164, 165
Wolverton 164
Woodford Halse 162, 245, 251
Woodhead tunnels 250
Worcester & Birmingham canal 158
Worcester Shrub Hill 148
works *see* railway works
World War II 19, 46, 53, 104
Worting 112, 115
Wrexham 122, 138
Wyatt, Digby 104, 108
Wrexham 122, 138
Wyatt, Digby 10

Y

Yarmouth 170
York 195, 205

AUTHOR'S ACKNOWLEDGEMENTS

When this series of railway books was launched in 2004 with *Branch Line Britain*, it was always our intention to produce one entitled *Along Main Lines*. It has taken a while, but it has now finally appeared, as number seven in the series. The process of planning the book and finding the illustrations has been, as usual, demanding, unpredictable, frustrating but generally enjoyable. By the nature of the subject, this book probably includes more pictures of trains than others in the series, something that no doubt will please some readers. However, this aspect has presented particular challenges to my editor, Sue Gordon, and my designer, Dawn Terrey, neither of whom can really be called railway enthusiasts. For this reason, I am more than usually grateful to them. Indeed, without their dedication, patience and support, this book could never have appeared. My wife Chrissie, even less of a railway enthusiast, has not only used all her great computer skills to make the illustrations as good as possible but has also had to live with me, and all things railway, during the long production process.

Particular thanks are also due to Barry Jones and Tony Harden, friends, fellow enthusiasts and great collectors, always ready to share those collections and their knowledge. Many other friends and colleagues from the railway world have also been helpful, but I owe a particular debt to Charles Allenby, Janet & Godfrey Croughton, and Dennis Wilcock of the Great Central Railway.

Finally, the support and enthusiasm offered by Neil Baber, and others at David & Charles, has been invaluable.

PICTURE CREDITS

The photographs used in this book have come from many sources. Some have been supplied by photographers or picture libraries, while others have been bought on the open market. In the latter case, whenever possible photographers or libraries have been acknowledged below. However, many such images inevitably remain anonymous, despite attempts at identifying or tracing their origin. If photographs or images have been used without due credit or acknowledgement, despite our best efforts, apologies are offered. If you believe this is the case, please let us know, as we would like to give full credit in any future edition.

Unless otherwise specified, all archive photographs and postcards are from the author's collection.
l = left; r = right; t = top; b = bottom; m = middle

Photographs by Paul Atterbury:
23tl, 23tr, 23br, 35b, 80b, 81t, 81ml, 81br, 102tl, 102b, 103br, 105ml, 106mr, 107t, 107m, 107b, 108t, 108b, 109t, 109bl, 109br, 130t, 130m, 130b, 131t, 131b, 154t, 154m, 154b, 155t, 155b, 176t, 176b, 177t, 177b, 199tl, 199tr, 199b, 222t, 222m, 222b, 223t, 223m, 223b, 234–35, 236t, 236b, 237t, 237bl, 237br, 238t, 238b, 239t, 239m, 239b, 240t, 240bl, 240br, 241t, 241b, 244t, 245t, 245b, 246t, 246m, 246b, 247m, 247b, 248t, 248b

Other photographs by:
DA Anderson 215b
WJ Verden Anderson 228b
Michael Baker 206b
SV Blencowe 122bl, 122br, 137mr, 137b, 244b
ML Boakes 14b
Peter F Bowles 87tl
Melvyn Bryan 83mr, 147b
MS Burns 213t
DE Canning 75br
IS Carr 105t, 189t, 193b, 212tr
Jim Carter 6tr
HC Casserley 95b, 168b, 184t
Revd AC Causton 98b
Rex Christiansen 132b
CRL Coles 159m
Colourail 87mr, 94t, 96tr, 98t, 114t, 123t, 124tr, 144tr, 168tr, 184b, 214b, 233b
JA Coltas 128t
K Connolly 15t, 73t, 75t, 87b, 103ml, 153b, 193t
Stanley Creer 143t
Derek Cross 59mr, 60t, 61br, 82b, 83tl, 97t, 115t, 145b, 190t, 196m, 200b, 201m, 205b, 213b, 215t, 216m, 216b, 217b, 229t, 229b
J Davies 143b
PA Dobson 147t
M Dunnett 206tl
Rick Eborall 251m
TJ Edgington 220b

Brian Edwards 147m
Mike Esau 106br, 110b
Kenneth Field 146t, 189b, 195t, 195b, 198t, 204tl, 204tr, 207t, 207ml
TG Flinders 195m
PJ Fowler 73m, 73b, 74b, 75bl, 79b, 84b, 149t
C Gammell 68b, 103tr, 105b, 168t, 171t, 172b
JG Glover 146b
John Goss 71b, 95t, 116b, 161ml, 188b, 190b, 191b, 192tl, 201t, 214tl, 228t
N Hamshere 98m
Clive Hanley 251br
Tony Harden 9br, 16m, 24bl, 24br, 25bl, 25br, 26mr, 27ml, 32tl, 33tr, 44tl, 44b, 45tl, 45b, 48tl, 62br, 63tl, 63tr, 63bl, 64tl, 64ml, 64mr, 80tl, 80tr, 80m, 82tl, 82–83, 85m, 88t, 89mr, 89b, 91ml, 102tr, 110tl, 110tr, 113ml, 113bl, 116t, 117t, 117m, 119ml, 119mr, 119bl, 126t, 127t, 127ml, 127mr, 129m, 132tl, 132tr, 133t, 133ml, 133mr, 133b, 134t, 135t, 138b, 139t, 139ml, 139mr, 139b, 151t, 162t, 162m, 163t, 163b, 165t, 165ml, 165mr, 172t, 175m, 178tr, 179br, 181t, 181ml, 181mr, 181bl, 185t, 185ml, 203m, 208tl, 226t, 227tr, 230t, 231t, 231ml, 231mr, 231b, 243mr, 243br, 244ml, 244mr, 245m, 247t, 248m, 249t, 249m, 249b, 250ml, 250b

Brian Haresnape 69t
Tom Heavyside 161tr, 192tr, 201b
GF Heiron 2–3, 68t, 72t, 77b, 78, 144b
RW Hinton 196b
Alan A Jackson 72b
FO Jotway 70–71m
Raymond Keeley 198bl, 198br
GD King 115m
Michael Mensing 6–7b, 7m, 49bl, 111b, 122t, 123b, 124tl, 124mr, 125t, 125b, 128b, 134b, 136t, 136b, 137t, 137ml, 148t, 148b, 149b, 150t, 152t, 152m, 153t, 158b, 159t, 159b, 162b, 170t, 170m, 170b, 171b, 180b, 182b, 183m, 185mr, 226b
Brian Morrison 94b
GR Mortimer 76b
ER Morton 157b
John K Morton 74t, 83tr, 191m, 205m
OS Nock 212tl
Ken Nunn 178b
RB Parr 220t, 221m
Ivo Peters 71t, 79t, 87tr
C Plant 74m, 161b
RCAHMS 232tl © Crown Copyright RCAHMS. Licensor www.rcahms.gov.uk
CA Richardson 91b
RC Riley 13b, 84t, 85t, 99t, 126b, 152b, 160tr
G Rixon 100b
RF Roberts 46b

Gerald T Robinson 50t, 86b, 99b, 115b, 204b
Peter J Robinson 214tr, 229m
PE Ruffell 207b
P Rutherford 112t
EA Sawford 209bl
Tony Sparks 251bl
NE Stead 96b, 196t
Stephen Tallis 197t
FM Tomlinson 203b
Eric Treacy 6bm
B Watkins 193m, 197bl, 197br, 202t, 205t, 217t, 221b, 227m
ER Wethersett 215m
TE Williams 70t, 70b
E Wilmshurst 113t
T Wright 47t

Chapter opener illustrations
Pages 234–5: The Camel Trail was built on the riverside trackbed of the former North Cornwall line from Wadebridge to Padstow. The opening pages of other chapters feature classic railway postcards and children's book illustrations from about 1905 to the 1960s.